THE TRINITY IN A PLURALISTIC AGE

The Trinity in a Pluralistic Age

THEOLOGICAL ESSAYS ON CULTURE AND RELIGION

Edited by

Kevin J. Vanhoozer

WILLIAM B. EERDMANS PUBLISHING COMPANY
GRAND RAPIDS, MICHIGAN / CAMBRIDGE, U.K.

© 1997 Wm. B. Eerdmans Publishing Co.
255 Jefferson Ave. S.E., Grand Rapids, Michigan 49503 /
P.O. Box 163, Cambridge CB3 9PU U.K.
All rights reserved

Printed in the United States of America

02 01 00 99 98 97   7 6 5 4 3 2 1

Library of Congress Cataloging-in-Publication Data

The Trinity in a pluralistic age: theological essays on culture and religion /
edited by Kevin J. Vanhoozer.
p.   cm.
Papers of the Fifth Edinburgh Dogmatics Conference
held in Edinburgh, Aug. 31–Sept. 3, 1993.
Includes bibliographical references.
ISBN 0-8028-4117-1 (pbk.: alk. paper)
1. Trinity — Congresses.   2. Religious pluralism — Congresses.
3. Religious pluralism — Christianity — Congresses.
4. Multiculturalism — Congresses.   5. Christianity and culture — Congresses.
I. Vanhoozer, Kevin J.   II. Edinburgh Conference in
Christian Dogmatics (5th: 1993: Edinburgh)
BT111.2.T76   1997
231'.044 — dc20   96-43912
                                                              CIP

Contents

CONTENTS

Preface

Each of the papers in this collection originated in the Fifth Edinburgh Dogmatics Conference on "The Trinity in a Pluralistic Age," organized by me under the auspices of Rutherford House and held in Edinburgh August 31–September 3, 1993. I am grateful to the main speakers and seminar leaders as well as to the participants who contributed to the discussions and who confirmed, by their diverse interests and concerns, that trinitarian theology offers fruitful perspectives on a pluralistic age. I would also like to express my gratitude to the Reverend David Searle for dealing with the administrative and logistical work so capably, thereby allowing the rest of us to concentrate on dialogue and doctrine.

KEVIN J. VANHOOZER
New College
University of Edinburgh

The Three-in-One and the Many

KEVIN J. VANHOOZER

The doctrine of the Trinity is what basically distinguishes the Christian doctrine of God as Christian, and therefore what already distinguishes the Christian concept of revelation as Christian, in contrast to all other possible doctrines of God or concepts of revelation.

Karl Barth, *Church Dogmatics*

The time is now well past when one could with any credibility assert the validity of one's own religion without reference to the truth claims of other religions.

N. Ross Reat and Edward F. Perry, *A World Theology*

Religious communities are likely to be relevant to the degree that they do not ask what is practical or relevant, but instead concentrate on their own intratextual outlook.

George Lindbeck, *The Nature of Doctrine*

It is bad to arrive too quickly at the one or at the many.

Plato, *Philebus*

One of the most challenging aspects of the contemporary situation for theologians is plurality, religious and otherwise. It is almost twenty years now since John B. Cobb wrote his *Christ in a Pluralistic Age*,[1] and the centrifugal forces pulling modern "metanarratives" apart show no sign of abating. Postmodern thinkers are suspicious of both comprehensive systems that claim to offer universal explanations and "grand narratives" that purport to tell the One True Story behind everyone else's story. The "greatest story ever told" is no exception; many pluralists include the gospel among those narratives that have worked their totalitarian oppression of other voices. Insofar as the Christian story too has repressed difference, it has failed to be a story of liberation. For many pluralists, the hegemony of the gospel in the Western world is a tragic tale of the one swallowing up the many.

The situation in postmodernity is otherwise. Today it is the many that threaten to swallow up the one. In disciplines as diverse as sociobiology and literary theory, and in biblical criticism, hermeneutics, and theology too, pride of place is accorded to particularities and differences. The various books of the Bible are all said to have their own theologies, and the search for a unity among the diversity has become increasingly problematic. A similar proliferation of perspectives and theologies characterizes the work even of so-called systematic theologies. What used to count as disinterested scholarship representing the universal viewpoint of reason and knowledge is today considered to be only one more particularity: the ideology of modernity.

But need the incontestable empirical fact of plurality lead one to embrace pluralism as a worldview? What is the place and function of the doctrine of the Trinity in an age of religious pluralism? Does the triune God have other names? Are there vestiges of the Trinity in other religions? And in an age in which many are seeking one theology to fit all the religions, does the Trinity constitute something of an intellectual scandal? Is there room for a doctrine of the Trinity in a global theology? If the one true God is also the triune God, might there not be a nonrepressive way of preserving differences within an overall unity?

The following papers respond constructively to these and other related problems. Our working hypothesis is straightforward, but its implications are immense: the doctrine of the Trinity, with its dual emphasis on oneness and threeness as equally ultimate, contains unexpected and hitherto unexplored resources for dealing with the problems, and possibilities, of contemporary pluralism. Indeed, it may be, as John Milbank has recently suggested, that the Trinity provides the only ontological ground for a harmonious reconciliation rather than a violent repression of the plurality that so marks our age.[2]

1. John B. Cobb, Jr., *Christ in a Pluralistic Age* (Philadelphia: Westminster Press, 1975).
2. John Milbank, *Theology and Social Theory* (Cambridge, MA: Blackwell, 1991).

· 1 ·

The Trinity as Public Truth

LESSLIE NEWBIGIN

By using the phrase "public truth," I am not suggesting an attempt to create (or return to) any kind of Christian theocracy. That would be mistaken even if it were possible. But I do not believe either that we can remain content with a situation in which trinitarian faith is merely a tolerated private opinion while other beliefs monopolize public debate. I can indicate what I have in my mind by using the image that Richard John Neuhaus uses in his book *The Naked Public Square.* The Church once dominated the public square, which was the meeting place of the civil community. It has, by and large, withdrawn. But the public square does not remain vacant. Other beliefs, ideologies, worldviews now control it. It is not suggested that the Church should once again seek to monopolize or dominate the public square. But we should insist that Christian doctrine, with its prime model in the doctrine of the Trinity, ought to be playing an explicit and vigorous part in the public debate that makes up the life of the public square.

The dominant voice in the public square, as far as our society is concerned, is an ideology of freedom that assumes that human freedom can be secured only by asserting total human autonomy in a manner that excludes the effective authority of God. Public debate in "modern" society is effectively atheist. Nothing has made this more vividly clear in recent years than the furor arising from the publication of Salman Rushdie's novel *The Satanic Verses* and the anger that erupted in the Muslim community. For Muslims blasphemy is a terrible crime, for God is a reality. For the intellectual establishment in this country the Muslim outcry could be seen only as an attack on freedom. If the word "blasphemy" has any meaning at all, it is understood to be merely an "in word" for the small minority of people who claim to believe in God.

1

Insofar as the public debate includes any reference to God, the reference is certainly not to the Blessed Trinity. In the ears of the vast majority of people, the word "God" certainly does not evoke the thought of the triune God. The public image of God is unitarian. And this is, of course, not new. I remember a visit to the ruins of Fountains Abbey in Yorkshire, when, as we walked from one part of the site to another, a friend read the relevant text from the official guide at each point. When we reached the ruins of the Chapter House, the text was as follows: "Here the monks gathered every Sunday to hear a sermon from the Abbot, except on Trinity Sunday, owing to the difficulty of the subject."

I must confess also that in my own theological training the doctrine of the Trinity played a very minor part. Of course it was not denied or questioned, but it had no central place. As I entered into the discipline of theological studies, the doctrines that gripped me, that glowed warmly in my mind so that I wanted to preach them, were concerned with grace, reconciliation, the kingdom of God, and the last things. In the *magnum opus* of my revered theological teacher, John Oman, there is no reference to the Trinity.

In my own experience, trinitarian doctrine came alive when I read classical scholar Charles Norris Cochrane's book *Christianity and Classical Culture* (1940). It is a study of the movement of thought from Augustus to Augustine, from the zenith of classical culture to its eclipse. Cochrane showed me how the trinitarian doctrine provided a new paradigm for thought, which made possible the healing of the dualisms that classical thought had been unable to overcome — the dualism between the sensible and the intelligible in the world of thought, and between virtue and fortune in the realm of action. The doctrine of the Trinity, in other words, was not a problem, but the solution to a problem that classical thought could not solve.

Whatever one may think of Augustine's theology in general and of his trinitarian doctrine in particular, he is important as standing at the point of transition from the world of antiquity to that world which was to become Western Latin Christendom. He is also, sadly, important insofar as he represents an early stage of the break between Eastern and Western Christendom. In his Confessions he tells us that as a schoolboy he hated Greek. Is it possible that, if this had not been so, Western Christendom would have retained a much stronger sense of the triune nature of God such as has remained characteristic of Eastern Orthodoxy?

Obviously the development of the doctrine of the Trinity was not the result of any kind of theological speculation within the tradition of classical thought. It was the result of a new fact (in the original sense of the word *factum*, something done). God had done those things that are the content of the good news that the Church is commissioned to tell, the gospel. This fact required a complete rethinking of the meaning of the word "God." One could, of course, decline to believe the "facts" alleged in the gospel. This is always a possibility. But if one believes that they are true, then this has to be a new starting point for thought. It is not something that can be fitted into existing models of thought — theological or metaphysical. Everything has to be rethought from the foundation upward.

All systematic thinking has to accept something as given, as data, as starting point. By definition a starting point is not a position that one reaches by the process of reasoning, but rather the place at which one begins the process of reasoning. The things to which the apostles bore witness had to be either disbelieved or else taken as a fresh starting point for thought. Nothing would be excluded from this rethinking. Even the most hallowed traditions about the meaning of the words "God," "man," and "history" had to be rethought on the basis of faithfulness to the record. From that long and very difficult exercise of rethinking came the new understanding of what we mean when we say "God." Everything depends upon a starting point — namely, the apostolic records accepted in faith. As Augustine said, we believe in order to understand.

For nearly a thousand years — the years that shaped the barbarian tribes of this western extension of Asia into a cultural entity that we call "Europe" — it was this way of thinking that shaped public discourse. The liturgy, the preaching, the drama, and the art of Christendom all took this apostolic record as the framework within which public discourse took place. But then a far-reaching shift took place. The classical tradition, especially as represented in Aristotle, had found a new home. Nestorian Christians, who carried the gospel into great stretches of central Asia, Arabia, and India, had translated Aristotle into Syrian. When the Arab armies overwhelmed the Christian church of the East, Christian scholars became the teachers of their overlords. Aristotle was translated into Arabic, and Aristotelian rationalism became an integral part of Muslim theology. By the end of the first Christian millennium, Islam was a more developed civilization than Western Christendom. During the period of intense mixing of Christian, Jewish, and Muslim culture in the Iberian peninsular, Aristotle was translated into Hebrew and Latin; and when, in the twelfth and thirteenth centuries, some of the great Muslim commentaries on Aristotle were translated into Latin, the effect on Western Christendom was profound and far-reaching. This way of thinking presented a penetrating challenge to biblical ways of thought.

3

A first Christian reaction was the banning of Aristotle from the University of Paris. But that could not be the last word. The work of Thomas Aquinas, which would shape the thought of Western Christendom to this day, was to effect a synthesis between the Aristotelian and biblical ways of thinking. Part of the cost of the synthesis was the acceptance of a duality in the way we come to know. Aquinas made a sharp distinction between those things that are to be known by the use of human reason, unaided by divine revelation, and those things that can be known only through faith in a divine revelation. Among the former was the existence of God; among the latter were such matters as the incarnation, the atonement, and the Blessed Trinity. One can say, therefore, that what Augustine had held together Aquinas had put asunder. Faith is no longer *the* way to knowledge; it is one of two alternative ways: there are things that we can know by the use of reason, other things that we can know only by faith.

This putting asunder has two substantial consequences. The first is that the God whose existence is proved by the use of unaided reason is not recognizable as the God who encounters us in the Bible, and certainly not the Blessed Trinity. We are faced with a problem that troubles us to this day. Which is the true God? Is the God of "natural theology" the true God, and the God of the Bible a distorted rendering of this God through the anthropomorphic imagination of simple believers? How is it conceivable that this God should be a baby in a manger or a man on a cross? And, above all, what is one to make of the Trinity? No wonder that it was hard to preach on Trinity Sunday! Or, on the other hand, is the God whom we encounter in the Bible the true God? In that case, what do we make of the God of natural theology? Must we not conclude that this is a construct of the human mind, an image thrown upon the clouds in the manner of Feuerbach's "Brocken-spectre" — in other words, an idol? That problem is still with us. Its relevance to our present discussion is obvious. Insofar as the word "God" makes its occasional entry into the discourse of the public square, it is certainly not the triune God. Is it unfair to suggest that it is much more recognizable as a conflation of Aristotle's prime mover with the Allah of the Qur'an?

The second consequence of the duality of the ways of knowing is as follows. If it is the case that divine revelation in Jesus Christ is not by itself a sufficient basis for confidence, if it requires validation from "The Philosopher," that is, by the unaided exercise of human reason, then the proofs for God's existence must be certain. We cannot afford doubt at this point where our final salvation is at stake. But it is notorious that the proofs are by no means certain. They are vulnerable. Skepticism about these proofs

4

could not be silenced. According to the Jesuit theologian Michael Buckley, when we come to the fifteenth century, skepticism was the dominant mood among intellectuals in western Europe. It was in this climate of skepticism that the young French philosopher René Descartes received, in 1628, from the Roman Cardinal Berulle, a commission to use his philosophical method to provide an irrefutable proof of the existence of God.[1]

Descartes's method involved three stages. Begin with a self-evident and indubitable truth, build on it with logical arguments having the clarity and certainty of mathematics, and separate what can be thus known with indubitable certainty from what is not certainty but mere belief. Descartes may thus be said to have completed the putting asunder of what Augustine had regarded as a unity. We have become accustomed to a sharp separation between a kind of knowledge that is certain and that can be expressed in mathematical terms (normally called "science") and all other claims to knowledge, which cannot be so formulated, such as claims to speak about beauty or goodness. The former kind of knowledge belongs properly to the public square. Claims to know what is good or what is beautiful have no place there; they are matters of personal belief, not of public truth. If some residual idea of God continues to haunt the public square, its form is certainly not that of the incarnate, crucified, and risen Jesus. It is the idea of a remote and shadowy figure that can play no part in the world of real "facts" with which science deals. And it certainly does not have the shape of the Blessed Trinity.

But it seems reasonable to argue, as some have done, that even this shadowy survival of a unitarian God in the area of public discourse corresponds to (and is perhaps responsible for) two very obvious elements in the reigning public truth.

One of these is our prevailing individualism. If the ultimate reality is this solitary, monarchical God, it is natural (some have argued) to think that human beings are essentially separate individual units, to be understood in terms of their individual selfhood and not, in the first place, as members in society. In this way of thinking, the autonomy of the individual self is the highest value, and the business of politics is to safeguard and extend this individual freedom against the pressures of the collective. It is true, of course, that this way of thinking does not go unchallenged. It has been said (by Dr. Harold Turner) that there are really only three fundamental "root paradigms" among human societies, which he calls the "atomic," the "oceanic," and the

---

1. Michael Buckley, S.J., *At the Origins of Modern Atheism* (New Haven: Yale University Press, 1987), pp. 71-73.

"spider's web." The first is that which seeks to explain everything in terms of its smallest units. Things are understood by analyzing them into their smallest parts. Matter is ultimately a collection of atoms. Society is a collection of individual human beings. The oceanic view sees things in terms of their ultimate unity. All rivers finally run into the same ocean. All roads lead to the top of the same mountain. In the end, there is only the one. The third model is the spider's web. Nothing is understood except in its relation to other things. Relatedness is the clue to the understanding of reality. This "root paradigm" is perhaps typical of Africa, as the oceanic is typical of India. It could be said that the atomic (individualist) model has been typical of "modernity" but that, as its inadequacies become more apparent, "postmoderns" are taking to the ocean — not least in the various manifestations of the New Age. If, as is said, the unitarian model of deity responds to, and perhaps encourages, the atomic view of human society, plainly the trinitarian understanding of God, in which relatedness is constitutive of the divine being, corresponds to a view of society that understands the human person in his or her relatedness to others.

The other way in which a unitarian model of deity may correspond to and perhaps influence human society is in respect to the role of power. Jürgen Moltman[2] has suggested that the unitarian model tends to validate patterns of domination in human affairs. A model of ultimate reality in terms of a monarchical figure of unlimited power tends — it is argued — to validate a conception of human affairs in which sheer power is the ontological basis of everything. Those who argue in this way can point to the influence of a kind of evolutionary theory that sees all things in terms of the battle for survival and supremacy, a view reflected in the horrifying escalation of violence as a normal part of life in "modern" societies. Against this, it is argued, a trinitarian understanding of God provides us with an ontology of love to replace an ontology of violence. The ultimate reality is the eternal mutual self-giving-in-love of the three persons of the Blessed Trinity.

We are witnessing at the present time a strong revival of trinitarian thinking in Western theology, and I suppose that the two lines of thinking that I have sketched have some part in encouraging this revival, as well as other factors such as the growing influence of Orthodox theology in the ecumenical movement. Clearly a fully trinitarian understanding of God as part of the discourse of the public square could change the terms of that discourse. But, just at this point, I think we have to be aware of a possible danger. Those who are familiar with developments in the ecumenical movement in general, and

2. Jürgen Moltman, *The Trinity and the Kingdom of God* (London: SCM Press, 1981).

with the work of the Faith and Order Commission of the World Council of Churches in particular, will know that *koinonia* has become the word that evokes the widest reverberations. It is the theme of the last report of the Anglican/Roman Catholic International Commission (ARCIC), and it was the theme of the recent world conference at Santiago de Compostello. It is also the central theme of the recent book by the new general secretary of the World Council of Churches, Dr. Konrad Raiser — *Ecumenism in Transition.*[3] In his book Dr. Raiser speaks of what he calls a paradigm shift in the ecumenical movement. He describes the paradigm shaping the movement up to the 1960s (the WCC Assembly at Uppsala in 1968 being the turning point) as "Christocentric universalism," and celebrates its replacement by a trinitarian paradigm. The Christocentric model is seen as unacceptable because it carries the message of lordship, of control from one center. "The Lordship of Christ over the Church and the World," the title of one of W. A. Visser 't Hooft's works, is indeed a title that captures the central thrust of the ecumenical movement during the formative years of the World Council of Churches. Raiser sees the quest for structured organic union among the churches as an implication of this. By contrast he looks to a more convivial, participatory model of unity. In this he correctly represents a strong thrust in contemporary Western society against all forms of elitism, paternalism, and domination, and in favor of the participation of everybody in the ordering of affairs. The goal of human existence is *koinonia,* the participatory fellowship of the entire human race, and in Raiser's vision the Bride coming down from heaven is not the *ekklesia,* but the *oikoumene.* It is obvious that a trinitarian understanding of God corresponds to this vision of *koinonia* as the goal of human existence.

What gives ground for anxiety here is the positing of a trinitarian model *against* the model of Christocentric universalism. The doctrine of the Trinity was not developed in response to the human need for participatory democracy! It was developed in order to account for the facts that constitute the substance of the gospel. It is the work of Christ in his incarnation, in his atoning work in death and resurrection, and in his bestowing the gift of the Holy Spirit upon the Church that made it necessary to undertake a radical reunderstanding of the being of God. To set a trinitarian paradigm over against a Christological one, and to commend it as corresponding to an egalitarian climate of opinion, would surely be a disastrous mistake. It is the work of Christ to bring us sinful human beings into the communion of the

3. Konrad Raiser, *Ecumenism in Transition: A Paradigm Shift in the Ecumenical Movement* (Geneva: World Council of Churches, 1991).

7

Blessed Trinity in such a way that as those who have been made members of the body of the Son by the work of the Spirit we are enabled to address the Father as "our Father." This *koinonia* is indeed the very being of the Church as a sign, instrument, and foretaste of what God purposes for the whole human family. But the sonship we have been given through the atoning work of Christ is defined in the gospel as both love and obedience. The consubstantiality of the Son and the Father does not exclude the obedience of the Son to the Father. "If you keep my commandments you will abide in my love, just as I have kept my Father's commandments and abide in his love."[4] The *koinonia* into which we are called through the work of Christ is not a kind of egalitarianism. "If I, your Lord and Master, have washed your feet, you also ought to wash one another's feet."[5] This is not egalitarianism, which is in fact one manifestation of individualism. This is a unique relationship that is made possible precisely by the fact that there is one who is Lord, whose lordship is expressed in servanthood, and who brings us into a community in which there is both obeying and being obeyed, a community in which love and obedience mutually interpret one another.

The Church learned to worship God as Trinity only because through the atoning work of Christ men and women have been brought to know Jesus as Savior and Lord and have been enabled by the gift of the Holy Spirit to be incorporated into the eternal offering of love and obedience of the Son to the Father. A trinitarian understanding of God cannot become part of public truth except through the acknowledgment of the universal lordship and saviorhood of Jesus Christ. To posit a trinitarian model as an alternative to the model of Christocentric universalism would surely be a grave mistake. The Trinity cannot be public truth except in the measure that the Church is faithful in its mission to the world. What troubles me, therefore, both about Konrad Raiser's book and about much talk that uses the word "ecumenical," is the reluctance to give any serious thought to the continuing mission of the Church to all the nations, an effective abandonment of their calling to preach the gospel to people of all races and creeds on the ground that it endangers human community. If the confession of Jesus as the one Lord and Savior of the world is withheld from the arena of public discourse and reserved for the privacy of the home and the sanctuary, then the only image of God present in the public square will be a unitarian one, whether the increasingly powerful image of the Allah of the Qur'an, or the shadowy and ineffective God of a Christendom that has lost its nerve.

4. John 15:10.
5. John 13:14.

8

• 2 •

Explaining Christianity to Pagans:
The Second-Century Apologists

GERALD BRAY

Introduction

The Apologists of the second-century Church were the first Christians to make a systematic attempt to enter into dialogue with the intellectual culture of the Greco-Roman world. The New Testament does not entirely ignore pagan culture, but references to it are scanty and cannot be said to constitute a coherent approach.[1] It was only later, when there were a substantial number of educated Gentile converts who felt the need to address the challenge of their own civilization, that an apologetic literature of this kind developed. From the surviving evidence, we know that it must have been widespread in the second-century Church, and its influence on the next generation of Christian writers was great.[2] The second-century Apologists did not consciously form a school of thought, and it is uncertain to what extent they borrowed from each other's work. Yet in spite of this they demonstrate a remarkable homogeneity in their patterns of thought, with only minor, and usually insignificant, variations among them.

By common consent, the greatest of these writers was Justin Martyr

---

1. Paul, although he called himself the Apostle to the Gentiles, seems to have spent most of his ministry among Diaspora Jews and "God-fearers" on the edge of the synagogues. Only in Athens did he engage with Greek culture (Acts 17:28), and when he referred to pagan philosophy, it was usually in a negative manner (cf. 1 Cor. 1:18–2:16).

2. See H. Chadwick, *Early Christian Thought and the Classical Tradition* (Oxford: Oxford University Press, 1966), pp. 1-30.

(c. 100–165), who has also left us the largest corpus of material. Next in importance come Theophilus of Antioch (fl. c. 160) and Athenagoras of Athens (fl. c. 177), both of whom left their mark on subsequent theological developments. Of lesser renown are Aristides of Athens (fl. c. 117–138) and the anonymous author of the *Epistle to Diognetus,* which for a long time was erroneously ascribed to Justin. All of these writers had in common the fact that they were Gentiles writing to fellow Gentiles, in the hope of persuading them to accept the truth of the Christian faith. It must be said at once that this hope was sadly disappointed; as far as we know, hardly anyone became a Christian as a result of reading one of these works, and the emperors and other high officials to whom they were addressed seem to have paid little or no attention to them. There is, however, some evidence that the Platonic philosopher Celsus had read at least Justin, and was angered by his attacks on pagan culture.[3] This suggests that some intelligent pagans felt threatened by what the Apologists were saying; but if this is true, the main effect was to strengthen their desire to oppose the new faith, not to persuade them to embrace it. The intellectuals were the last social group to be attracted to Christianity in great numbers, and many were never converted. Even two centuries after the triumph of the Cross, Athens still had schools of Platonic philosophy, which disappeared only when Justinian forcibly closed them down in 529.

But if the Apologists failed to persuade the pagan intelligentsia to convert to Christianity, what success did they have? The main answer to this seems to be that they provided the young Christian Church with an intellectually respectable apologetic in the face of a still-dominant paganism. They taught and encouraged a generation of Christian theologians who succeeded in establishing Christianity in the forefront of contemporary intellectual activity. It was on the foundations laid by men like Justin that Irenaeus, Tertullian, Clement of Alexandria, and, finally, Origen were able to erect a Christian theological edifice that was equal to the task of challenging and eventually supplanting the dominant philosophies of the late Roman world. These later giants elaborated on the arguments of the Apologists and integrated them into much more ambitious theological systems of thought, but they said little that was fundamentally new. It was in the writings of these second-century Christians that the main lines of the

3. Chadwick, p. 22: "There is a strong case for thinking that Celsus had read some Christian apologetic writing, and that he may well have been especially provoked by Justin." The point has been argued in great detail by C. Andresen, *Logos und Nomos* (Göttingen, 1954), though some of his conclusions seem a little dubious; see Chadwick, p. 133.

Christian intellectual assault on paganism were laid down, to remain largely unchanged until paganism itself was suppressed.

The conclusion that the Apologists wrote mainly for the Church, in spite of appearances to the contrary, and that their greatest success was among those who already shared their basic presuppositions, not among those who fundamentally disagreed with them, imposes itself readily enough, and few modern scholars would doubt it. On the other hand, it is generally believed that the Apologists had a genuine sympathy for certain elements in the pagan culture that rejected them, and that their writings were a serious attempt to forge some kind of synthesis out of the Bible and the best of Greek philosophy. Their failure to communicate with intellectual pagans was therefore not so much their fault as the unfortunate result of a deep-seated pagan prejudice that claimed that there were no educated Christians.[4] In this paper it is our intention to reexamine this belief and to demonstrate that the Apologists were not nearly as well disposed toward Greek intellectual culture as has often been supposed, and that their writings, far from being a polite attempt to enter into dialogue with non-Christians, were in fact an aggressive attack on all forms of paganism, which was all the more telling because of the Apologists' knowledge of the strengths and weaknesses in their enemies' presuppositions and arguments. They were evangelists rather than diplomats, and their primary objective was to win converts to the Christian faith, not to find ways in which that faith could be integrated into the prevailing culture of the time.

The Two Conflicting Worldviews

The first and most fundamental line of attack that the Apologists used was their conviction that Christianity, which was directly dependent on its Jewish predecessor, was a more ancient religion than anything known to the Greeks, whose best ideas had all been cribbed from the Old Testament. The clearest statement of this view was given by Theophilus,[5] but it was common to all the Apologists. As Tatian put it:

> We ought to believe Moses, rather than the Greeks, because he is so much older. Without properly understanding them, the Greeks drew on Moses' teachings as from a well. For many of the philosophers among them,

4. See Chadwick, p. 24.
5. Theophilus, *Letter to Autolycus* III, 20, 29.

stimulated by curiosity, endeavoured to corrupt whatever they learned from Moses and from those who have philosophised like him. In the first place, they wanted people to think they had something of their own to offer, and second, they wanted to misrepresent the truth and turn it into a fable by covering up in rhetoric whatever they did not understand.[6]

This position was basically taken over from the Jews, who had argued along similar lines.[7] It is easy to find fault with it, and Celsus, the great second-century adversary of Christianity, was not slow to do so. His response was simple — the affinities between Christianity and paganism were to be explained in exactly the opposite way. It was not the Greeks who had borrowed from Moses, but the Christians who had stolen the pure ideas of the philosophers and turned them into a religion![8] Today we realize that this argument was futile, and that both sides were fundamentally mistaken, but in the second century things were not so clear. Some pagans were prepared to accept that Plato could have read Moses,[9] and the ancients' habits of plagiarism were such that no acknowledgment would have been expected.

What a modern reader notices immediately is that neither side seems to have imagined that Plato and Moses could have come to the same conclusions independently. To them it was axiomatic that one must be derived from the other, and it was this belief that made Christians so determined to prove the antiquity of their religion. For if it could be demonstrated that the Greeks had discovered an idea long before Christianity even existed, then Celsus's claim that Christianity was a corrupt form of Hellenism would be immeasurably strengthened. To understand the mentality of both the Apologists and their pagan opponents, we have to go back to the basic nature of Greek civilization, on the one hand, and of the Judeo-Christian tradition, on the other. Both cultures held the view that all human beings are rational, and therefore capable of understanding the rational principles underlying the universe, but both also believed that in actual fact this understanding was reserved to a chosen few.

Both the Greeks and the Jews thought that they were a special people, set apart from the rest of the human race. Within the Greek world, the philosophers constituted an élite of those who regarded themselves as the

---

6. Tatian, *The Address to the Greeks* 40.
7. Josephus, *Contra Apionem* 2, 169.
8. Origen, *Contra Celsum* 1,4.
9. Numenius of Apamea was one; he was quoted to that effect by Clement of Alexandria (*Stromateis* 1,150,4).

truly enlightened, possessing an innate right to rule over others. In the Jewish world there had been a number of self-appointed spiritual élites, but these had mostly disappeared after A.D. 70, leaving only the Christians, who soon moved away from the remnants of organized Judaism almost entirely. But in cultural terms, Christians stood in much the same relationship to Jews as the philosophers did to ordinary Greeks. Both appeared as the enlightened element of a special people, the true interpreters of an ancient tradition that claimed the exclusive right to interpret ultimate reality.

Of course, it was just this structural similarity that made the two groups mutually exclusive, and this is the real key to understanding the nature of their interaction. Neither side could deny that the other's views had some merit, but to understand that as anything other than a corrupt borrowing of their own tradition would have been to surrender a basic principle: that they, and they alone, had direct and pure access to the source of truth. It was therefore impossible for either the Apologists or Celsus to accept pluralism, in the sense of allowing that truth may be derived from more than one source. All that they could do was to point out the degree to which the other side had perverted true knowledge in the course of the borrowing process.

We may demonstrate this by taking an extreme, but not atypical, example from Justin, who believed that Plato had some inkling of the crucifixion of Christ. He derived this extraordinary idea from a phrase in the *Timaeus*, which reads: "He placed him crosswise in the universe." According to Justin, Plato got this from the account of the brass serpent in Numbers 21:8, which Jesus used to refer to his crucifixion (John 3:14). By any standard this connection is far-fetched, especially when we remember that Plato used the letter *chi* ("in the shape of an x") and not *stauros*,[10] and that elsewhere Justin insisted that pagans had not picked up on the crucifixion, which was meaningless to them.[11] But none of this stopped Justin, who went on to link Plato's remark to his supposed intuition of the Trinity:

> Plato read these things (about the brass serpent) but did not understand them accurately. He did not realize that it was the figure of the cross, and so he said that the power next to the first God was placed crosswise in the universe. And as to his speaking of a third, he did this because he

10. Justin, *Apology* I, 60. The quote is from Plato, *Timaeus* 36 b-c.
11. Justin, I, 55.

read, as we said above, what was spoken by Moses: "that the Spirit of God moved over the waters." He thus gives second place to the *Logos* which is with God, who he said was placed crosswise in the universe, and the third place to the Spirit who was said to be borne upon the water, saying: *ta de trita peri ton triton* (the third things around the third one).[12]

The extreme obscurity of these references did not bother Justin in the least; as far as he was concerned, it was further proof that even the brightest of the philosophers really understood next to nothing of the truth. As he went on to add:

It is not that we hold the same opinions as others, but that they all speak in imitation of us. Among us these things can be heard and learned even from illiterate people, who are uneducated and barbarous in speech, but wise and learned in mind.[13]

This remark brings out an essential difference in the nature of the two competing élites. The Greek philosophers relied on education as the cachet that guaranteed entry into the charmed circle of the elect, but the Christians put little faith in human knowledge. Quite apart from the fact that much of the learning on which pagans prided themselves was either false or immoral (or both),[14] the Christians believed that true enlightenment was spiritual, and not merely intellectual. The Christian élite was open to any and every true believer, whether educated or not. This assertion is of the utmost importance in evaluating the Apologists' attitude toward pagan intellectualism. In the light of statements like these, the common belief that they respected pagan intellectual achievement and sought to imitate it cannot be sustained. The so-called anti-intellectualism of a man like Tertullian, which scholars like Etienne Gilson have tended to regard as somewhat aberrant,[15] was altogether typical of the period, and representative not of anti-intellectualism as such, but of opposition to the form in which "learning" had presented itself in the Greek world before the coming of the Gospel.

---

12. Justin, I, 60. The quote is from a spurious letter attributed to Plato, *Ep.* 2.312e.
13. Justin, I, 60.
14. Aristides went into this in the greatest detail; see, e.g., *Letter to Hadrian* 2.
15. See E. Gilson, *Reason and Revelation in the Middle Ages* (New York: C. Scribner and Sons, 1938).

The Attack on Pagan Religion

In mounting their attack on pagan religion, the Apologists were able to count on the support of many intellectual pagans who were disgusted with the immorality and absurdity of much of what passed for religion in the second century. Aristides[16] went into the pagan pantheon in great detail, dividing the gods into different cultural types. The Chaldeans, whom he calls simply "Barbarians," worshipped creatures instead of the Creator, a sure sign that they could not even protect their own divinity, but allowed themselves to be identified with things they had supposedly made. The Greek gods were even worse, because they were humanized, with the result that men were led into immoral behavior in imitation of the gods. Greek mythology was also contradictory, making it impossible to devise a consistent picture of the heavenly beings. Worst of all were the Egyptians, who turned animals into gods and even practiced incest as a sacred rite. For all these reasons, the charge of atheism made against Christians for their failure to recognize the pagan gods was fully justified, a point that Justin also made as follows:

> We are called atheists, and we confess that we are atheists, so far as gods of this sort are concerned, but not with respect to the most true God, the Father of righteousness and temperance and the other virtues, who is free of all impurity. We worship and adore both him, and the Son who came forth from him . . . and the prophetic Spirit, knowing them in reason and truth.[17]

The assertion on the part of Christians, as well as pagans, that the former were atheists as far as ancient paganism was concerned, demonstrates that there was no conceptual link between this kind of religion and Christianity. There is not even an attempt on the part of the Apologists to identify the biblical God with one or other pagan deity. Zeus, as the chief of the gods, would have been the obvious choice, but although Justin was prepared to admit that like the true God, Zeus was capable of nonsexual procreation, he was quick to add that both he and his sons were well-known fornicators — a remark that instantly invalidated the earlier comparison![18]

The general view was that pagan gods were evil spirits,[19] and it was

16. Aristides, *Letter to Hadrian* 2.
17. Justin, I, 6.
18. Justin, I, 21.
19. Justin, II, 13.

15

the Apologists more than anyone else who gave the word *daimōn* the negative connotation it now has. Justin went into more detail about them than did the other Apologists, and even claimed that the pagan gods were the offspring of fallen angels and human women. His assessment of them is worth quoting:

> But the angels transgressed, and were captivated by the love of women, and gave birth to children who are called demons. Afterwards they subdued the human race to themselves, partly by magical writings, partly by fears and the punishments they occasioned, and partly by teaching them to offer sacrifices . . . which they needed after they were enslaved by lustful passions. Among men they sowed murders, wars, adulteries, intemperate deeds and all wickedness. The poets and mythologists did not realize that it was the angels and the demons begotten by them who did these things . . . and so they ascribed them to God himself, and to those reckoned to be his offspring.[20]

A favorite source of examples of the kind of deception pagans had fallen into was the way in which they had misread the Old Testament and made up their own myths from it.[21] According to Justin, pagan temples practiced a form of ritual washing analogous to baptism, which they had supposedly got from Isaiah 1:16-20,[22] and pagans also had a habit of setting up images of Persephone at springheads, because they had misunderstood the moving of the Spirit of God over the face of the waters in Genesis 1:2.[23] However, these apparent similarities between pagan practices and the biblical record were regarded as evidence of pagan stupidity, not of their residual wisdom, as can be seen from what Justin says about them:

> In imitation of what is said about the Spirit of God moving over the waters the demons said that Persephone was the daughter of Zeus. And in a similar way they craftily pretended that Aphrodite was the daughter of Zeus, not by sexual union, but, knowing that God conceived and made the world by the Word, they say that Aphrodite was the first conception *(ennoia)*, which we consider to be very absurd, because they produced the conception in a female form.[24]

20. Justin, II, 5.
21. Justin, I, 54.
22. Justin, I, 62.
23. Justin, I, 64.
24. Justin, I, 64.

To regard the divine form as female was for Justin the height of folly — a sure sign that the pagan world was still walking in its primeval darkness! Pagan religion derived much of its mythology from Greek poetry, and so it is significant that Theophilus roundly condemned both Homer and Hesiod, whom he regarded as nonsensical.[25] Only Athenagoras managed to put in a good word for Euripides and Sophocles, and then it was only because they apparently believed, like the philosophers, that God was a unity.[26]

A curiosity is that the Apologists seldom said anything about fate, which in pagan religion was a force superior even to the gods. The one exception to this was Tatian, who tackled the problem head-on and denied that fate existed. According to him, sin was an act of free will, and to blame it on fate was to abdicate responsibility for it. As he said:

> How is it that you are fated to be sleepless because of greed? Why are you fated to grasp at things often, and often to die? Die to the world, repudiating the madness which is in it. Live to God, and by knowing him, lay aside your old nature. We were not created to die, but we die by our own fault. Our free will has destroyed us; we who were free have become slaves; we have been sold through sin. Nothing evil has been created by God; we ourselves have manifested wickedness; but we who have manifested it are able again to reject it.[27]

Tatian clearly had no temptation to identify fate with the Christian concepts of divine sovereignty and predestination; as far as he was concerned there was no link at all between what pagans believed and what the Christian Gospel proclaimed to be true.

The Attack on Pagan Philosophy

When we turn from pagan religion to pagan philosophy, we expect to find a more sympathetic approach on the part of the Apologists. After all, Plato too had disapproved of poetic mythmaking, and had wanted to ban both poetry and religion from his ideal republic. The philosophers also preached morality in a way that pagan religion did not, and this also drew them closer to Christians. Likewise, the appeal to reason was one that both

25. Justin, II, 5-6.
26. Athenagoras, *Embassy, or Plea for the Christians*, 5.
27. Tatian, *The Address to the Greeks*, 11.

philosophers and Christians could share, and might lead them to form some affinity with each other. Lastly, the leading Apologists seem to have been converted to Christianity in the course of their philosophical searchings. This was certainly true of Aristides and of Justin, and it was probably true of Athenagoras as well. Aristides in particular made his own reflections as a philosopher an important part of his argument for Christianity. In his *Epistle to Hadrian* he expected the emperor to swallow the following description of God, more or less without argument:

> God is not born, not made, an ever-abiding nature without beginning and without end, immortal, perfect and incomprehensible. When I say he is perfect, I mean there is no defect in him; he is not in need of anything, but everything needs him. . . . He is neither male nor female. The heavens do not limit him, but the heavens and everything, visible and invisible, receive their bounds from him. He has no adversary, for no one is stronger than he is. He does not have wrath or indignation, because nothing can withstand him. He has no ignorance or forgetfulness, for he is wisdom and understanding, and everything that exists stands fast in him. He demands no sacrifice or libation . . . or anything else, because all living creatures stand in need of him.[28]

This, let it be said at once, was the common ground between Christians and their philosophically educated opponents, and it is immediately apparent just how close they were on many matters of fundamental importance. From statements like this, it is hardly surprising that the belief that the Apologists looked favorably on Greek philosophy is widespread in academic circles today. Henry Chadwick's view may be regarded as typical in this respect:

> Of all the early Christian theologians Justin is the most optimistic about the harmony of Christianity and Greek philosophy. For him the gospel and the best elements in Plato and the Stoics are almost identical ways of apprehending the same truth.[29]

Later on, Chadwick mentions that according to Justin, Socrates was a Christian before Christ, on the ground that "all rational beings share in the universal Logos or Reason who is Christ."[30]

Still later, Chadwick declares:

28. Aristides, *Epistle to Hadrian*, 1.
29. Chadwick, pp. 10-11.
30. Chadwick, p. 16.

Justin does not merely make Socrates a Christian. His Christ is a philosopher, 'no sophist', but a genuine teacher of the way to 'happiness' *(eudaimonia),* in himself the personification of 'right reason' *(orthos logos)* teaching 'divine virtue'. His teaching in the Sermon on the Mount is wholly in line with natural law; it is a universal morality, valid for all races and stripped of the national particularism of Judaism.[31]

Here we have as good a summary as it is possible to get of the prevailing scholarly attitude toward Justin, and by extension toward the other Apologists as well. An examination of the texts in question however, reveals that Chadwick's rosy picture is more than a little idealized. Let us begin with the question of Socrates. What Justin said was this:

> We have been taught that Christ was the First-begotten of God and we have indicated above that he is the Logos of whom all mankind partakes. Those who lived by reason are Christians, even though they have been considered atheists, such as, among the Greeks, Socrates, Heraclitus, and others like them.[32]

First, let us note that although Justin allowed that all men partake of the Logos, who is Christ, that was not the reason why Socrates could be called a Christian. A Christian was one who lived by reason, which is not at all the same thing as being a rational creature. What Chadwick has inadvertently omitted is the reality of sin, which entails humankind's enslavement to demonic forces that prevent them from realizing the goal of their creation. Justin did not make that mistake, and lamented the fact that the ideal of a truly rational existence was unattainable after the Fall.[33] Socrates and Heraclides were honorary Christians, not because they were philosophers, but because they were persecuted for their lack of belief in the pagan theological system. Justin made this very clear:

> Those who were born before Christ assumed human nature were dragged into law courts as irreligious and meddling persons, when they tried in human narrowness to think out and prove things by reason. Socrates, the most ardent of all in this regard, was accused of the very crimes that are imputed to us. They claimed that he introduced new deities, and rejected the state-sponsored gods. But what he did was to ostracize Homer and the other poets, and to instruct men to expel the evil demons

31. Chadwick, p. 17.
32. Justin, I, 46.
33. Justin, I, 10.

and those who perpetrated the deeds narrated by the poets; and to exhort men by meditation to learn more about God who was unknown to them, saying: "It is not an easy matter to find the Father and Creator of all things, nor, when he is found, is it safe to announce him to all men."[34]

Justin then went on:

Yet our Christ did all this through his own power. There was no one who believed so much in Socrates as to die for his teaching, but not only philosophers and scholars believed in Christ, of whom even Socrates had a vague knowledge (for He was and is the Logos who is in every person . . .).[35]

So although Socrates was the greatest of the Greeks, even he had only a vague knowledge of Christ, which was all that the innate Logos could reveal to a person without the revelation of the gospel. Using the common philosophical language of the day, Justin referred to this indwelling Logos by the term *logos spermatikos,* and he did not hesitate to admit that Plato and the Stoics did the best they could with it. However, to conclude from this that Justin had a positive attitude toward the inheritance of Greek philosophy is a misreading of the facts. What Justin said was this:

When I learned of the evil camouflage which the wicked demons had thrown around the divine doctrines of the Christians to deter others from following them, I had to laugh at the authors of these lies, at the camouflage itself, and at the popular reaction. I am proud to say that I strove with all my might to be a Christian, not because the teachings of Plato are different from those of Christ, but because they are not in every way similar; neither are those of the other writers, the Stoics, the poets, and the historians. For each one of them, seeing, that through his participation in the seminal Logos *(logos spermatikos),* what was related to it, spoke very well. *But they who contradict themselves in important matters evidently did not acquire the unseen, heavenly wisdom and the indisputable knowledge. . . . Indeed, all writers, by means of the engrafted seed of the Logos which was implanted in them, had a dim glimpse of the truth. For the seed or something and its imitation, given in proportion to one's capacity, is one thing, but the thing itself, which is shared and imitated according to his grace, is quite another.*[36]

34. Justin, II, 10.
35. Justin, II, 10.
36. Justin, II, 13.

From this extensive quotation we can see clearly what Justin's true position was. As far as he was concerned, the world was blinded by the encompassing power of the demons, who had almost completely obscured the truth. Relying on the *logos spermatikos* within them, pagan writers and philosophers strove to overcome this darkness, with varying degrees of success. But only those who renounced it to the point of sacrificing their own lives could be said to have achieved their goal, and even then they were putting their trust in something they did not fully understand. At the end of the day there was only one way to know the truth — by God's grace, which reveals it to sinful man. As Justin said in conclusion, to have the capacity to know is one thing, but actually to know is something else again!

As for the notion that Christ was a philosopher, Justin nowhere said this. The full quotation, to which Chadwick makes a passing reference, reads as follows:

> Christ's sayings were brief and concise, for he was not a sophist, but his word was the power of God.[37]

Nor is it accurate to say that Justin believed that the Sermon on the Mount is wholly in line with natural law. What he actually said was:

> God shows every race of man that which is always and in all places just, and every type of man knows that adultery, fornication, murder, and so on are evil. Though they all commit such acts, they cannot escape the knowledge that they sin whenever they do so, except those who, possessed by an unclean spirit, and corrupted by bad education and evil habits and wicked laws, have lost (or rather have stifled and stamped out) their natural feelings of guilt. . . . I am of the opinion that our Lord and Savior Jesus Christ very aptly explained that all justice and piety are summed up in these two commandments: "Thou shalt love the Lord thy God with thy whole heart, and with thy whole strength, and thy neighbour as thyself."[38]

This shows that Justin believed that every human has some knowledge of good and evil, though that may have been corrupted by various factors, and that Jesus responded to that in his teaching. It does not mean that Justin believed that pagans understood the teaching of Jesus before he gave it, nor that unaided reason could ever have come to as perfect a knowledge

37. Justin, I, 14.
38. Justin, *Dialogue with Trypho*, 93.

21

of the truth before divine revelation appeared. Chadwick, and along with him the majority of modern scholars, has reconstructed a picture of Justin's relationship to pagan philosophy that is altogether too positive and encouraging. What he and others have ignored is Justin's strong insistence on the reality of corruption, induced as often as not by demonic forces, which has obscured the light of natural law and reason, and rendered the attempts of pagan intellectuals to recover it null and void. A person who, like himself before his conversion, relies on them for guidance is walking in the dark without any hope of coming into the light by his or her own efforts.

Where Chadwick is right, however, is in his assertion that Justin was the most positive of the Apologists toward Greek philosophy. Theophilus of Antioch said that the philosophers had an absurd notion of God because they did not distinguish the Creator from his creation. According to them, both God and matter were uncreated![39] This negative note is sounded also by Tatian, who launched a bitter attack on Greek philosophy at the very beginning of his *Address*. Neither Theophilus nor Tatian disputed the idea that the right use of reason would lead to a knowledge of God, but they both claimed that it was precisely this that the philosophers lacked. Justin may have been more polite than they were, but it is hard to see that he held a very different opinion from theirs!

What Christianity Had to Offer the Pagan World

In defending the superiority of Christianity to all forms of paganism, the Apologists stressed above all the moral standards that were prevalent in the churches of their time. The confidence with which all the Apologists used this argument is truly astonishing; it must mean that the standard of discipline within the Christian community was extremely high. Justin argued that Christian morality was required by the moral character of God,[40] an attribute that made him far superior to any pagan deity. Justin, like Tatian and others of their time, sounds Pelagian to our ears, because he said things like "God accepts only those who imitate the virtues which reside in him" and "those who choose what is pleasing to him are, because of their choice, deemed worthy of incorruption and of fellowship with him," but we must be careful not to detach him from his context. His point was that Christian behavior reflected the being of God, and that there was a necessary

39. Theophilus, II, 4.
40. Justin, *Apology*, I, 10.

22

connection between these two things. The source and motive of Christian morality was faith, a point on which even the purest Augustinian would be agreed, and beyond that Justin did not probe.

Athenagoras regarded the argument from morality as so telling that he used it twice.[41] Aristides recognized that morality was a trait that Christians shared with Jews,[42] but he went on to argue that Jewish worship was inferior because Jews worship angels rather than God. It is not clear on what misunderstanding that remark is based, but it evidently was meant to carry weight with pagans. Probably Aristides was sensitive to the developed angelology of contemporary Judaism, which went hand in hand with its contemporary apocalyptic tendencies.

Another powerful argument was the assertion that Christians worship the Creator and not creatures. This was stated bluntly by Aristides,[43] and developed at some length by Tatian.[44] Tatian argued that the Logos was the uncreated agent of Creation and that man possessed the same principle of immortality because of his rational nature. However, he was careful to insist that man will not attain immortality unless he is united with the Holy Spirit.[45] Athenagoras likewise said that Christians distinguish God from the material world[46] and that they do not worship anything in the created universe.[47]

The main question that has to be asked about the method used by the Apologists is whether they built on what they believed to be right and good in paganism, or whether they thought that Christianity was a totally new religion that had little or nothing in common with what had gone before. None of them had a good word to say about pagan religion, which they regarded as both illogical and immoral. These views were common among educated pagans, many of whom were just as disgusted as Christians were with what they saw going on in the pagan shrines. Aristides was able to assume without argument that the Emperor Hadrian would share his general concept of God; the difference between the two men was that Aristides could put a name to the Supreme Being and worship him, whereas Hadrian was confined to an abstract philosophical principle. Justin was able to appeal to the principles of Roman justice in favor of the Christians,

41. Athenagoras, 11, 32-34.
42. Aristides, 14.
43. Aristides, 15.
44. Tatian, 4-7.
45. Tatian, 12-14.
46. Athenagoras, 15.
47. Athenagoras, 16.

pointing out that they were charged with crimes of which they were not guilty, and condemned merely for professing the name of Christ.[48] The illogicality of this behavior was meant to be a particularly powerful argument among the well educated, because it demonstrated an inner inconsistency in their own ethical standards.

But the fact that even Justin regarded pagan philosophers as inconsistent demonstrates that he did not seriously believe that it was possible for a pagan to find Christ by pursuing an intellectual path. Aristides is the only one who came close to arguing that on the basis of his own experience, though it is important to remember that he was speaking from hindsight. The good elements in Greek philosophy fell into place once Christianity was understood and adopted; they were not sufficient on their own to lead people into the way of truth. The reason for this was that humankind was in the grip of Satan and his angels. It was not merely intellectual ignorance, but spiritual slavery that had to be dealt with if humans were to be saved and truly enlightened. It was Justin who made this point most clearly when he concluded the First Book of his *Apology* with a short discourse on the necessity and the importance of Christian baptism.[49] Without baptism there could be no illumination of the mind, so that even the most clever philosopher is lost in pagan darkness. Without baptism, there was no cleansing of the soul, so that the plague of immorality remained to haunt the unbeliever, however much the unbeliever might pretend otherwise. It was baptism that broke the power of the demons, and made it possible for a person to begin a new life as a child of God. Baptism, which only the Christian Church could offer, was thus presented as the only way in which a Gentile could enter into the grace of God in Christ, however much the Gentile may have learned from the presence of the Logos in him or her.

In the final analysis, therefore, the Apologists were not forerunners of the kind of religious dialogue advocated by pluralists in our own time. However much they may have agreed that all human beings possessed something of the divine Logos, and even when they were prepared to commend a man like Plato for having made the best use of the Logos given to him, pagans were still the victims of demonic deception, with only a partial (and usually misleading) grasp of the truth. Intimations of the Trinity in their writings were so obscure as to be almost meaningless; Plato stumbled upon a trinitarian view of the universe by accident, and had no idea of the significance of his "discovery," if that is the right word for it. It

48. Justin, *Apology*, I, 3.
49. Justin, *Apology*, I, 61.

24

would be more accurate to say that even he did not worship the Father correctly, because he did not distinguish the Creator from his creatures. Nor did he worship the Son, because he completely misunderstood Moses' reference to the crucifixion. Nor indeed did he worship the Holy Spirit, because the Spirit's life-giving power was not present in him.

As far as Justin was concerned, it was baptism that underscored the fundamental character of the Christian, as one who was born again in Christ. Such a person had the spiritual equipment necessary to distinguish the true from the false in paganism, but in making this distinction he was only bringing out the blindness of the Greek philosophers even more clearly. For when all was said and done, the philosophers lacked the spiritual perception needed to distinguish right from wrong, and so were corrupted even in their better moments. This was a far cry from accepting that paganism had something positive to offer, or that it was possible to become a Christian without renouncing one's former life. Christ came into the world to judge paganism, even in its noblest forms. Whatever differences of approach there were among the Apologists, their basic message was the same — only by repentance and rebirth could a human see the kingdom of God.

The Trinity and "Other Religions"

STEPHEN WILLIAMS

The Contemporary Interest

The designation "other religions" in the title is deliberately loose. These days, we are often urged to speak of "religious traditions" rather than "religions" and further urged not to lump together non-Christian religious traditions under that word "other." I am not challenging these points. The title of this paper simply announces its intention economically, namely that of remarking on aspects of Christian belief in God as Trinity in connection with non-Christian religious traditions.

Connections are certainly made these days. Over two decades ago, Raimundo Panikkar published his book *The Trinity and the Religious Experience of Man*.[1] It was described by Rowan Williams as "one of the best and least read meditations on the Trinity in our century."[2] Bishop Williams said this in an essay responding to a more recent contribution by Panikkar, which appeared in 1987 in the collection of essays edited by Hick and Knitter under the title *The Myth of Christian Uniqueness*.[3] Williams's own essay on the Trinity was one of three by three different contributors that

1. Raimundo Panikkar, *The Trinity and the Religious Experience of Man* (London: Darton, Longman and Todd, 1973).
2. Rowan Williams, "Trinity and Pluralism," in Gavin D'Costa, ed., *The Myth of Christian Uniqueness Reconsidered: The Myth of a Pluralistic Theory of Religions* (Maryknoll, NY: Orbis, 1990), p. 3.
3. John Hick and Knitter, eds., *The Myth of Christian Uniqueness* (Maryknoll, NY: Orbis, 1987).

opened a volume written in response to Hick and Knitter's and titled *The Myth of Christian Uniqueness Reconsidered.*[4] But as a sustained attempt at a trinitarian theology in the context of global religion nothing seems to equal the work that appeared just three years ago by Ninian Smart and Steven Konstantine, *Christian Systematic Theology in World Context.*[5] The Trinity and the religions is thus a theme of contemporary interest, and the above are only examples.[6] We shall set the stage with some general remarks on Panikkar and Smart.

For Panikkar, the Trinity is able to provide us with a pattern for making sense of divergent spiritualities on the historical religious scene. Consider what is suggested by the following: we encounter belief in an indescribable ultimate ground; there is conviction of a personal dialogical relationship with the ultimate; and people experience the fathomless depth of their own being. Now the Christian belief in God as Trinity embraces belief in a transcendent principle, a personal manifestation, and an immanent ground of all things. Such a belief suggests how the various spiritualities described may be possible and all have their grounding in an ultimate. Here a concept rooted in the Christian theological tradition has a wider explanatory function, but concepts rooted in non-Christian theological traditions can illuminate that selfsame Christian notion. For example, Advaitic Hinduism sophisticatedly proposes that God and the world are not strictly one and identical but are certainly not two and separate. God and world is or are neither one nor two. One must refuse to unite or to separate in an arithmetically styled ontology. Now such a conceptuality serves to do what the Christian theological tradition tries to do when it refuses to ascribe either a single or a tri-separate identity to the *personae* of the Trinity.[7] Here we have an example, then, of religions mutually enriching each other's self-understanding.

Smart and Konstantine adumbrate a "neotranscendentalist, pluralistic, social Trinitarian, panentheism embedded in a soft epistemology."[8] In this context, Smart, like Panikkar, explores conceptual connections between Christian trinitarian and non-Christian thought. An example of how he sets it up is the following:

4. D'Costa, ed., p. 3.

5. Ninian Smart and Steven Konstantine, *Christian Systematic Theology in World Context* (London: Marshall Pickering, 1991).

6. My attention was recently drawn to A. Pieris, e.g., *An Asian Theology of Liberation* (Edinburgh: T & T Clark, 1988), p. 62.

7. I am following Panikkar's book rather than essay here.

8. Smart and Konstantine, p. 441.

We can make a distinction too between the non-relational and the relational aspects of the Trinity. There is, first, the infinite of the divine life as it circulates through the selfless spirits. This is the non-relational aspect. Then, second, there is the plurality of the three Persons. Third, there is the communal life — the shared ego of the three. These last two aspects are relational (the first to one another, the second towards creatures).[9]

In Eastern thought, nonrelational aspects of the ultimate are often comprehended independently of the relational ones. Such is the case in Taoism, Vedantic Hinduism, and Zen Buddhism. Less abstractly, one may say that "Spirit" is comprehended and apprehended as a symbol of peace and bliss in Pure Land Buddhism. This is not so distant from Panikkar's objective in identifying spiritualities. And like Panikkar, Smart pushes the possibility of using extra-Christian conceptuality to illuminate the Trinity. The phrase "selfless spirits" in the above citation translates the Buddhist *anatta*, which functions well as a conceptual explanation. Smart typically "mixes" his terms: Christians believe that "Brahman," who can be called "she," is incarnate; the Father is the *antaryamin* ("inner controller") of the cosmos as the Spirit is of conscious beings and as the Son (as *avatar*) is of the personal identity of Jesus.[10]

One striking feature of both these contributions is the absence of any discussion of the question of criteria. The criteriological question that must be answered is this: what enables something to count as a formulation of the doctrine of the Trinity? Here, Panikkar and Smart take their place in an inheritance that has ignored some sharp questions put to trinitarian theologians by Michael Durrant.[11] Durrant some time ago argued that belief in God as Trinity is incoherent. At the end of his argument, he faced the obvious criticism that at most what he had shown was that specific formulations of Christian belief in God as Trinity are incoherent. The doctrine itself was not directly under threat. In response, Durrant pressed the objector to identify what constitutes the essence of such belief apart from its formulation; what exactly the formulation is a formulation of; how one judges whether a given formulation is a formulation of the doctrine of the Trinity and not the formulation of another (one's own) doctrine. Whatever may be held to be defective in Durrant's contribution, he rightly

9. Smart and Konstantine, p. 174.
10. Smart and Konstantine, p. 236.
11. Michael Durrant, *Theology and Intelligibility* (London: Routledge & Kegan Paul, 1973).

forced the question of criteria. How do we justify a claim that we have offered a reformulation of the doctrine of the Trinity as opposed to offering something different? Panikkar and Smart use trinitarian vocabulary and triadic patterns, but never once address, let alone answer, this question.

It may seem that such a challenge threatens to reduce discussion to the level of semantics and misses out on discussion of the substance and usefulness of the proposals in question. But the failure we have identified is more widely significant. Let us take Smart's work. From his conceptual presentation of the ontology of divine life, Smart moves naturally enough to ask about the way a religion might grasp the relational or the nonrelational aspects of divine life. It is vital to see what is going on here. In patristic trinitarian theologies, language was used to express in some way concrete relations held to obtain between concrete *hypostases* or *personae,* as they came to be called. If there is anything relational or nonrelational in the divine life, it is of these particular hypostatic relations or this particular substantial entity that we make such predications. But when one conceptualizes these relations in relatively abstract terms, what happens? Concrete relations are presented relatively abstractly in the form of what I shall provisionally call *ideas.* Then the question of whether religious philosophies grasp the *ideas* in some ideational form threatens to be identified with the *separate* matter of whether the religious experience expressed in those philosophies is an experience of God. This is the price one pays for ignoring the criteriological issue.

Now if we wish to insist that a doctrine of the Trinity is irreducibly about concrete relations between Father, Son, and Spirit, this does not entail that it is impossible to benefit from extra-Christian conceptuality in its elucidation. Suppose we grant that in principle we may make theological use of an ontological insight that Plato possessed or conceptual distinctions that Aristotle offered. There seems no barrier, then, in principle, to the use of Indian or Far Eastern ideas in Christian theology. The fact that these come from what we can term "religions" rather than from Platonic or Aristotelian "philosophies" will be deemed an advantage by some, a disadvantage by others. But conceptual borrowing as such does not entail that Advaitic Hindus or Yogacarin scholars are having an experience of God, still less a saving one.

So much for questions of broad principle that arise from two distinguished contributions to the issues of interest. I do not, however, wish to limit discussion to these contributions. At the end of his book on *The Trinity and the Religious Experience of Man,* Panikkar says that he has been arguing for "a spirituality whose most simple expression would say: Man is more than 'man';

he is a theandric mystery."[12] Rowan Williams follows through Panikkar's proposals, building on them, though not uncritically. He reads Panikkar's enterprise as a scheme for discovering what constitutes the human good. And human good, as Williams puts it, lies in "the stature and fulness of Christ" as "what defines the most comprehensive future of mankind."[13] The concrete future is conceived "in terms of a Christlike humanity, humanity delivered from a slavish submission to an alien divine power and participating in the creative work of God."[14] It seems to me that this might not sound impressive to Taoists or Buddhists without a sense of being enslaved. And no more than the others does Williams address the criteriological issue. Yet both Panikkar and Williams indicate the broad context of their reflections on the Trinity. And the question of how a doctrine of the Trinity grounds a sound theological anthropology is very much in the air. It is consequently worth taking up here.

Trinity, Humanity, and Love

In the most recent book-length study of the doctrine of the Trinity, Ted Peters runs through recent contributions to trinitarian theology: Zizioulas, Jüngel, Boff, Moltmann, LaCugna, Pannenberg, and Jenson.[15] They all have in common the belief that we must understand the Trinity in terms of interpersonal personhood, and our own personal being is grounded in that. Very roughly, contemporary advocates of a doctrine of the Trinity are dominantly in favor of a form of social trinitarianism. That description, however, is a very broad one, for it covers historical and conceptually heterogeneous terrain all the way from the Cappadocians to Hegel. As regards the contemporary scene, we are urged to think of our personhood in relational terms, and the relations proper to our being are relations of love. The social being of the Trinity undergirds this. This way of thinking promises to establish an important connection between belief in the Trinity and the interpretation of religion, and Peters does include some discussion of these matters.[16] For religions strive to understand human beings and seem alike to prize love. The question that naturally suggests itself is this: does Christian belief in God as Trinity ground a plausible understanding

12. Panikkar, p. 82.
13. Williams, p. 9.
14. Williams, p. 11.
15. Ted Peters, *God as Trinity* (Philadelphia: Westminster, 1993).
16. Peters, pp. 73ff.

of humanness and human love more successfully than nontrinitarian religious thought? This is the question we shall explore from now on.

The first thing to consider is whether religions share any common ground in their understanding of humanness and of human love in particular or whether we have illicitly smuggled this assumption into the discussion. In his celebrated work *An Interpretation of Religion,* John Hick claimed that they do share something important to all concerned.[17] Hick argued that all the postaxial religions understand salvation as a shift from self-centeredness to Reality-centeredness. A Kantian humility prevents us from endorsing any particular claims to know the Real in itself, and the phenomenon of religions encourages us to hold that they grasp the Real under different appearances. What we do find in common is the conviction that *vera religio* bears fruit in *agape* or *karuna.* The principle known to Christians as the Golden Rule is religiously omnipresent.

Hick certainly believes that to be a person is to be related to others. But he does not derive that belief from a doctrine of the Trinity. The "Real" cannot strictly be personal, since being personal entails being related and we have no reasons for believing that the Real is eternally related. A doctrine of the Trinity is useful as a model for seeing how the One can be conceived under many aspects. But a modal trinitarianism is better than a social understanding for this purpose, and the Buddhist *trikaya* in any case does the job just as effectively.[18]

Hick's thesis about the unity of *agape/karuna* is deeply problematic. Ninian Smart remarks that "humility may loom large among Christians where the root sin is pride or ego-inflation: but it may not be important for Muslims or Brahmins and indeed may be thought counter-productive in a number of cultures."[19] We should take the point. This means that the phenomenon of *agape/karuna* is not unified in the way Hick suggests it is. Christian *agape* is quite inseparable from humility. If humility is placed in relation to love in anything like the diverse ways that Smart notes, the name "love" in the other cases designates different phenomena. No doubt the same point could be made in relation to "compassion" in a comparison of how "compassion" and "merit" are related in Christianity and Mahayana Buddhism.[20]

17. John Hick, *An Interpretation of Religion* (New York: Macmillan, 1989).

18. Hick, pp. 170ff.

19. Smart and Konstantine, p. 91.

20. This emerges very strikingly from a general study of Buddhism such as that of Peter Harvey, *An Introduction to Buddhism: Teachings, History and Practices* (Cambridge: Cambridge University Press, 1990).

Nevertheless, are there not still phenomenologically similar features across the ethical traditions of the religions? The English word "compassion" sounds more specific than "love" and can naturally be taken as one of the forms of love. Is compassion not both exalted and experienced universally or almost universally, not by all people but in all major religious cultures? Is this not much the same across the religions and indeed outside the religions too? This last question suggests that we cannot avoid introducing humanism into the consideration of religions. As a matter of fact, Hick himself is quite willing to connect religion and humanism with reference to ethical sentiment and action.[21]

A useful starter for discussion of this question is Arthur Schopenhauer's essay *On the Basis of Morality.*[22] Schopenhauer is of interest as the first major Western philosopher to turn explicitly eastward in a semiatheistic rejection of Western ethics. In the first part of his essay, Schopenhauer attacked the foundation of Kantian ethics. He found it defective on more than one score. The heart of the problem is that Kant makes rational obligation the fount of ethics, the imperative source of duty. According to Schopenhauer, this is an inverted form of the divine command, a rational "thou shalt" — "you ought." This does not wash, because morality springs from sympathy, not from duty. That is how it is with the empirical phenomenon of morality. Kant conducts his search for a moral imperative "after the first impetus and occasion for it had already been given by another, positively effective, real moral motive" (p. 74) that "proclaims itself unbidden" (p. 75) and springs from human nature. Kant's ethics is founded *not* on a vaunted fact of consciousness but on a constructed universal maxim. And the imperative to treat others as ends and not means is disguised egotism; it has an eye, in its Kantian formulation, on the consequences of not so doing; it is a hypothetical imperative in disguise — do this or you will be unfortunately treated.

The foundation of ethics is human nature, and only one thing gives moral worth to action: compassion. In compassion (a) the other's weal becomes mine; (b) I feel the other's woe as my own; (c) I identify with the other's woe. This is how natural compassion works in fact in humankind. Now a mystery attends this phenomenon. How is (c) possible? I feel the pain of the other as the other's pain, not my own, but it is truly I that feel it and I feel it truly. There is a "wholly direct and even instinctive partici-

21. Hick takes in almost everything, in fact; see the reference to Marxist-Leninism, Trotskyism, and Maoism in Hick, p. 306.
22. Arthur Schopenhauer, *On the Basis of Morality* (Indianapolis: Bobbs-Merrill, 1965).

pation in another's sufferings." That is *agape* "first theoretically mentioned, formulated as a virtue . . . by Christianity" (p. 163). At least that was how it was in Europe. Asia saw it long before, and saw it better. There it is named *karuna*. And it is Asia that finally solves for us the metaphysical puzzle of compassion, the ability to identify myself with the other. Kant actually helps us here. He held that space and time are ideal forms of cognition. If he is right, *plurality* is ideal; if plurality is ideal, the Real is One. The One appears in the Many. Indian religious philosophy in particular had tapped into this. It developed the idea that plurality was only apparent. There is only the One. So the conception that establishes the difference between the ego and the non-ego is erroneous. I am one with the other. That explains compassion. "This art thou" . . . this "bursts forth in compassion" (p. 210). Compassion, then, is a matter of identity. We have already established that action has moral worth only when I experience myself as fundamentally relational. Now we see that relationship must be understood as identity. Identity is the clue to our humanness and compassion.

Schopenhauer's response to Kant and his appropriation of oriental *karuna* put him on a collision course with Hick, who connects Kantian with religious ethics as follows:

> The fundamental moral claim . . . to treat others as having the same value as myself . . . in effect a transcription of the Golden Rule in Scripture . . . is likewise a translation of Kant's concept of a rational person as an end and of right action as action which our rationality, acknowledging a universal impartiality transcending individual desires and aversions, can be seen to be required.[23]

But whether or not Schopenhauer effectively succeeds in disconnecting what Hick here joins together, his own scheme, whatever its strengths, is flawed. The heavy reliance on Kant's doctrine of the ideality of space and time is not defended in the particular essay we have considered, and if one is not persuaded on that score one will not be persuaded by the philosophical reasons that Schopenhauer advances for celebrating Indian religious thought. But in any case, he falsely assumes that it is a phenomenological observation to say that we directly participate in the sufferings of another. It is not — not in the sense that Schopenhauer means it to be, as a report of human experience. "Direct" is an interpretation beyond the bounds of his phenomenology. What if I were to insist that all true compassion in a

---

23. Schopenhauer, p. 149.

relationship — as, indeed, all good things — is mediated by God the Holy Spirit? What *appears* "direct" is therefore not unmediated. The invisible bond of Spirit is the basic explanation of the phenomenon. The possibility of offering such an account indicates that Schopenhauer is indulging in metaphysical interpretation precisely where he says he is not.[24]

So Schopenhauer fails here, but he presents us with a good challenge. For here we have a powerful account of monistic identity as the ground of our humanness and human love. It does not matter whether or not Schopenhauer got his oriental religions right. Let us allow that compassion of the true and ordinary human kind that Schopenhauer has in mind is a sign of healthy interpersonal relational orientation. Is it better explicable on a trinitarian model than on Schopenhauer's philosophy of identity, spelled out in his own understanding of Eastern religions?

Now monistic philosophies of identity differ among themselves, as far as the untrained Western eye or untutored Western mind can tell. Despite the dangers in slapping the label "monism" onto various forms of Mahayana Buddhism, I shall do so for the sake of argument, for in fact nothing turns on the descriptive. Mahayana Buddhism is brought in for contrast with, let us say, a kind of Vedantic Hinduism that holds Brahman to be beyond good and evil. Schopenhauer believed that compassion springs from sheer human nature. But humanity is nurtured differently in different contexts. The untrained eye and untutored mind may well suspect that different modes or degrees of compassion will be nurtured in accordance with a sense, on the one hand, that reality is suffused with Buddha-nature compassion or, on the other, that reality is nondualistically beyond good and evil. It is immaterial whether or not this fairly characterizes a contrast between one strain of Hinduism and one strain of Buddhism. What matters is the idea that it is not a philosophy of identity as such but the *nature* of the ultimate as represented to consciousness that affects compassion. For in putting it like that we potentially distinguish between the nature and the form of the ultimate. And this is relevant when we consider the Trinity.

The charge is often made — and here Moltmann is among the leaders — that a monotheistic nontrinitarian monadic view of deity fosters asocial individualism. A social trinitarianism becomes the necessary basis here of healthy anthropology, if not in explicit opposition to perceived oriental monism, certainly in explicit opposition to a skewed nontrinitarian monadism, which Western monotheism is alleged to be. But the importance

---

24. The distinction between expounding the foundations of ethics and addressing the metaphysical question is fundamental to Schopenhauer's strategy in this essay.

of *Trinity* is considerably exaggerated here. The religion of the Old Testament is evidence of this. Whatever we may say in Christian reflection on the Old Testament view of God, God is not consciously appropriated as interpersonal Trinity in Old Testament religious experience. Yet both compassion and relation are vital. Why should I be compassionate? Because God is thus in His nature and has dealt with us thus. Community life is set up as the form of human life, with love as its principle. But while it may have been frequently believed that we are created in the image of God for community, it was not said that we are created for community because God is community and we are not bidden to love because of interpersonal trinitarian love. Yet Old Testament religion — whose various stages we may, of course, distinguish — throbs with the call for compassion and the sense of neighborly relationship. The more the prophets proclaim that there is one God, the more strident the call to mutual responsibility.

My argument here is tentative. It is true that the New Testament witnesses the emergence of ideas of God that plausibly support "social trinitarianism" of some form. It is true also that with the increasing vision of God, love intensifies in its light. But is it not the impress of the *nature* of God that grounds compassion and a sense of relationship and mutuality? If form is important, it is not trinitarian form in anything like the specificity of contemporary social understandings. There may be many reasons for preferring an interpersonal view of God to Schopenhauer's ideas as a ground for understanding humanness and human love. But to press the point about "social form" is to risk obscuring the Old Testament insight whose validity remains — namely, that it is a perception of the nature of God, holy, just, and merciful, that nourishes human love and community. Obviously devotees of this generalized notion, "social trinitarianism," fully emphasize nature, but they overemphasize the difference made by specific persuasion on "form."

This is quite emphatically *not* to say that belief in or the vision of God as Trinity makes no difference to my way of viewing my own or others' humanity. The love of God as Trinity is a love eternally expressed, his holiness, a holiness in which there is eternal acquiescence. The greatness of divine sacrifice is magnified when we think how out of their fullness, Father and Son turn outward. The greatness of divine salvation is magnified when we think how the Spirit as Person incorporates us into this fullness. And the greatness of divine unity is magnified when we think how the Spirit comes upon the Son and the Son sends the Spirit in undivided concord and fellowship. The call to us to submission and service and to the communion of love is incomparably enriched. In contrast, Hindu *bhakti* sounds superficial, not derived from a knowledge of the majesty and holiness of Father, Son, and Spirit and so not evincing "holy" concern for others. In trinitarian light, Buddhist compassion is lonely and inadequate, not founded in conscious living community with divine persons.

But such a perspective should be common to trinitarians and does not suppose an adjudication between Western and Eastern strands. It is a less conceptually conscious trinitarianism than is evidenced in an *insistent* socially trinitarian interpersonalism. Here one must heed Brunner. His view of the doctrine of the Trinity, far sharper and more developed in his *Dogmatics* than in his earlier work, *The Mediator,* is misunderstood if he is reckoned to be an opponent or only a reluctant upholder of the doctrine.[25] Brunner undoubtedly holds to belief in God as Trinity and holds it to be a vital tenet.[26] But he was unhappy with the speculative developments of trinitarian theology from Origen onward, with its ruminations on divine being rather than divine action. For Brunner, belief in the Trinity is the end term of our confession, not a subject for theological reflection in the name of church doctrine.

Brunner's discussion has its faults. It does not take into account the possibility of the kind of association of immanent with economic Trinity promulgated after his day by Karl Rahner. There is far too much confidence, to say the least, in the rhetorical claim that "no Apostle would have dreamt of thinking that there are three Divine Persons, whose mutual relations and paradoxical unity are beyond our understanding."[27] But he fires warning shots across the bows of any who advance to explore the relations of Father, Son, and Spirit. And he stays his thinking on the content of divine revelation as a revelation of divine love and holiness. Such is the revelation of that love and holiness that even when it was the unity of God that exercised the thought and vision of the prophets, it impinged with power on the matter of serving others in the spirit of the Father of compassion and holiness. If our understanding of humanness is enhanced by belief in God as Trinity, it is arguably not by pressing the social point but by pressing the trinitarian reality that this is achieved.[28]

25. Emil Brunner, *The Christian Doctrine of God: Dogmatics 1* (Cambridge: Lutterworth, 1949), ch. 16.

26. One needs, of course, to study Brunner's terminology very carefully here, but pp. 206-17 and the surrounding comments can scarcely be understood in any other way.

27. Brunner, p. 226.

28. We labor here under the difficulty provided by such a broad range of positions comprehended under "social trinitarianism." But its contemporary exponents frequently go beyond Brunner in their exposition of the doctrine, and the more it is felt that Brunner's

Certainly we can make a more general point here and caution against exaggerating the force of a "social" Trinity. Canon Allchin describes the way in which the doctrines of incarnation and social Trinity gained importance in Anglicanism in the last century, grounding a theology of social concern. He quotes as an example Thomas Hancock's 1869 sermon, *The Fellowship in God the Source of Humanity's Fellowship with God.*

> There is no certainty that God is the Father unless it be true that he has, and ever has had, a co-eternal Son. . . . St. Hilary baldly said: 'We could not preach one God to man, if we had to preach a lonely God'. . . . He who made us is not a cold, hard, lonely, self-amusing Mechanician, caring little what becomes of his experiments.[29]

The antithesis proposed here is unwarranted. It is one thing to deny Trinity in the name of the one God; it is another to characterize such a God as a "cold, hard, lonely, self-amusing Mechanician." Judaism stands as a witness to the false nature of this disjunction, whatever we may think *can* happen to sheer monotheism and however convinced we are that the Old Testament witness points to plurality in the Godhead. Even less would we seem warranted in comparing a nonsocial doctrine of the Trinity with a social doctrine along Hancock's line, to the disadvantage of the former.

There may be mileage in a theological attempt to show how a belief in God as "social" Trinity gives superior undergirding to a shared view of human relations and human compassion. And this is surely what a strong "social" trinitarian implies in relation to other religious traditions. There may be mileage, but we must not overestimate the fuel capacity. However, this is negative. Let us finally broach the positive.

Postscript

The doctrine of the Trinity elucidates the claims both to particular revelation and to universal presence that Christians have wanted to make on

---

position is not satisfying for its failure to explore inner trinitarian relations, the more the suspicion grows that speculative theology is aspiring to parity with the *kerygma*. It may well be that Brunner underestimates what exegesis will yield in support of a more detailed exposition of the Trinity, but he rightly sensed the danger of substituting a relatively developed concept for a *mysterium fidei*.

29. Quoted in A. M. Allchin, *The Kingdom of Love and Knowledge* (London: Darton, Longman & Todd, 1979), pp. 102-3.

behalf of a personal God. These claims can be set in the light of "other religions." It is true that the conviction that God is personal is effectively rejected by the radical "pluralist" approaches to Christianity and world faiths. Quite apart from what Hick says about the impossibility of eternal personhood, the logic of his general argument carries him away from belief in divine personhood. For he insists that we cannot know the Real *an sich* and that conceptions of the Real as impersonal are no less valid than conceptions of the Real as personal, as far as we can judge. Now at least one thing is clearly ruled out on Hick's account: the possibility of viewing God as a personal, effective, purposeful communicator. The Real has given no effective revelation of his reality as personal. For if there had been such an effective revelation, it would not be optional, but mandatory, so to regard the Real. If there is no such revelation, the Real is either unwilling or unable to reveal. If the Real is unwilling, then we may have a personal being, but one utterly unlike the personal deity of Christian belief. If the Real is unable, then we do not have a personal being at all in the sense conceived in Christian thought. On neither account is the Christian option open. Hick, therefore, is not really allowing that it is valid to think of God as personal provided that we concede that other ways are valid. He denies that we may validly think of God as personal in any way resembling the tradition. It has been difficult enough for many to swallow the claim that Christians must regard belief that God is personal as an optional belief. One is dealing with a veritable camel if one is to swallow the claim that such belief is no longer optional at all and that effectively impersonal notions of the Real are nearer the mark.

If, however, we do believe in a personal God, particular revelation is not the scandal that it is often thought to be in light of other religious traditions. How more effectively can a personal God communicate the truth about his nature than by appearing personally in the world, if that is possible? And how can personal appearance in the world be possible in its fullness unless God remains God in heaven while God is also God on earth? And how is that possible unless there are what we have come to call at least two persons? This is not an a priori argument about what is required by a self-revelation of personal deity. I am simply noting one feature in the theological logic of the claim that God is incarnate in a particular person.

The point can be developed further along the same lines. It is of interest to note that Smart retains the identity claim that a particular earthly person is identical with the Supreme Being *only* in the case of Jesus. His "pluralism," if we should call it that, is therefore unusual, although one would certainly need to examine the whole of his thought to interpret his claim properly at this point. What makes Smart say what he says is that he finds the notion of a God who does not suffer religiously intolerable and the notion of a God who suffers in his own person on earth, thus partaking fully of the human condition, eminently acceptable. Christianity alone makes this supremely morally acceptable claim about its God.[30] Some who refuse Smart's morally constraining presuppositions here may nevertheless speak of something else, the need for atonement in particular space and time. That belief has brought problems in its train particularly since the days of the early Socinians, but I note it in the shadow of Smart's insistence that the very particularity of divine action indicates the reality of divine universal being. In brief, in both versions God wants to accomplish something on this earth, and religiously this is an eminently fitting volition. Of course, one might opt for multiple incarnations to make this point. I think that some reflection will show the difficulties involved in positing several, frequent, and persistent incarnations for this purpose as opposed to the once-for-all.[31] This strengthens the point that personal appearance in particular space and time, far from denying the reality of a universally concerned personal God, seems precisely its apt expression. And according to the Christian notion of God as Trinity, the fullness of divine earthly "experience" and reality of divine earthly appearance is possible only on the assumption that a distinction exists between Father and Son.

Again, much has been made of the Spirit in the context of our knowledge of world faiths or global religious traditions. For example, we hear that God is not remote from any; His personal presence is "immediate," so that *God,* not some effluence, or deputizing power, is truly present to those of other faiths.[32] Karl Rahner's work, despite the widespread unease with "anonymous Christianity," remains a prominent influence in this area. Rahner found that only a view of Spirit that makes Jesus Christ savingly present throughout the world really does justice to the governing theological axiom: God desires the salvation of all.

30. Thus: "We affirm the identity statement that Jesus is God (and we do not make this statement about anyone else)" (Smart, p. 110) and worldly suffering makes "virtually necessary" the embodiment of the Divine (Smart, p. 431).

31. It is not possible to pursue this properly here. Two points, however, can be made. The first is that even the speculative mind surely boggles at the thought of multiple and successive incarnations of the same person happening all the time, with the identity questions that would raise. The second is that most cultures would still be left without the presence of God incarnate, as only one space could be occupied at any one time.

32. Gavin D'Costa is one of the leading figures influenced by Karl Rahner here; see, e.g., his essay, "Christ, the Trinity and Religious Pluralism," in D'Costa, ed., *The Myth of Christian Uniqueness Reconsidered.*

But even if one grants the axiom and understands it as does Rahner, in terms of active will, and takes the Spirit to be the universal presence of God in the world, one need not go all the way with Rahner. Indeed, his scheme is surely speculative at best. And even if one defends its theology, it is not the only way to believe in salvation outside explicit knowledge of Jesus Christ. One may believe it without being able to trace the operations of the Spirit in the world in their relation to the saving death of Christ. Without knowing the ways of God as Rahner does, we may still say that all good things come from God; that the Spirit is the form of God's immanent presence in the world; that the Spirit is fully and personally God. So we may say that God's world is not deprived of God himself, and the particularity of God's appearance in history is not the location of God in one rather than another space and time. So we may speak of the universal presence of God throughout a world inhabited by adherents of many faiths. And on a trinitarian view of God, the possibility of fully personal immanence along with personal transcendence and personal appearance is due to the reality of the personal being of the Holy Spirit alongside that of the Father and the Son.

As I have been occupied largely with Trinity, humanness, and religion, these remarks do not adumbrate a perspective so much as indicate its possibility. There is nothing novel in it. The suggestion is humdrum enough: the doctrine of the Trinity explains the ontological possibility of incarnation and immanence in a way that elucidates what has seemed to many the "exclusivity" of God, revelation, and salvation in Christian understanding. Whether one remains closer to the so-called exclusivist position or to the so-called inclusivist one is another question. But humdrum as it is, it announces a *prima facie* possibility for explicating the doctrine of the Trinity in the context of other faiths. Perhaps interpersonal Trinity has its possibilities too. It is those things that are *revealed* that belong to us and to our children and the things that are *revealed* that we must communicate to children of other faiths.[33]

33. This is Brunner's emphasis too.

4

Does the Trinity Belong in a Theology of Religions? On Angling in the Rubicon and the "Identity" of God

KEVIN J. VANHOOZER

Charting the Waters: The Problem of Identity and Difference

Rivers and bridges, for some reason, figure prominently in debates concerning religious pluralism and the theology of religions. Mahatama Gandhi was one of the first to use a river analogy: "One may drink out of the same great rivers with others, but one need not use the same cup"; "The soul of religion is one, but it is encased in a multitude of forms. My position is that all the great religions are fundamentally equal."[1] "Same . . . one . . . equal . . ." — do all religions refer to the same God? This question of whether the Christian God is identical with the referent of the other religions is, fundamentally, a question about the identity of God.

The Three Rivers

Raimundo Panikkar symbolizes the history of Christianity's relation to other religions by three sacred rivers. The Jordan, with all its historical

---

1. Cited in Bruce Demarest, *General Revelation: Historical Views and Contemporary Issues* (Grand Rapids: Zondervan, 1982), 255.

associations to the particular events of Israel with Yahweh and Jesus with the Father, stands for exclusivism — the traditional belief that Christianity is the only true religion. The Tiber symbolizes the distinctly Western mentality of Christendom, with its medieval Crusades and its modern missions. As all roads lead to Rome, so all rivers — religions — lead to Christianity. The "Declaration on the Relation of the Church to non-Christian Religions," approved by the Second Vatican Council in 1965, made inclusivism the official Roman Catholic position.[2] Inclusivists take the position that Christianity embraces what is true in the other religions.

According to Panikkar, neither mentality, Jordan or Tiber, adequately recognizes or respects the "otherness" of the other religions. The Ganges, formed from many sources and dispersed in diverging outlets, represents contemporary pluralism: Christianity is one of several valid religions. Here Panikkar wishes to speak neither of doctrinal Christianity nor of institutional Christendom, but of "Christianness": the mystical, spiritual core of the faith that is shared by humanity at large.[3] We will return to Panikkar, and his trinitarian solution to the problem of religious pluralism, in due course.

Bridges over the Theological Rubicon

Yet a fourth river has been invoked. Contemporary Christians, aware of the plurality of religions, stand before what Paul Knitter calls a "theological Rubicon": "To cross it means to recognize clearly, unambiguously, the possibility that other religions exercise a role in salvation history that is not only valuable and salvific but perhaps equal to that of Christianity. . . . It is to admit that if other religions must be fulfilled in Christianity, Christianity must, just as well, find fulfillment in them."[4]

Knitter notes three principal strategies — three "bridges" across the Rubicon — by which theologians typically move from exclusivism or inclusivism to a pluralistic position. First, an ever-increasing awareness of historical-cultural relativity with regard to knowledge and beliefs in general.

2. See David Wright, "The Watershed of Vatican II: Catholic Approaches to Religious Pluralism," in Andrew D. Clarke and Bruce W. Winter, eds., *One God, One Lord: Christianity in a World of Religious Pluralism* (Grand Rapids: Baker, 1992), pp. 207-26.

3. See Raimundo Panikkar, "The Jordan, the Tiber, and the Ganges," in John Hick and Paul F. Knitter, eds., *The Myth of Christian Uniqueness: Toward a Pluralistic Theology of Religions* (Maryknoll, NY: Orbis, 1987), pp. 89-116.

4. Hick and Knitter, p. 225.

Seen from atop this bridge, exclusivists and inclusivists alike appear presumptuous with their breathtaking truth-claims of Christian absoluteness. John Bunyan had at least a foot on this bridge when he wrote: "Every one doth think his own Religion rightest, both *Jews* and *Moors* and *Pagans;* and how if all our Faith, and Christ, and Scriptures, should be but a thinks-so too?"[5] The second bridge is theological: it is the awareness that the divine mystery exceeds our linguistic and conceptual resources. Christian formulations are not exempt; they afford no privileged access to the divine Fact. The third bridge, the shared concern for justice and human welfare, is ethico-political in nature and best expressed by Hans Küng: "no world peace without peace among the religions, no peace among the religions without dialogue between the religions, and no dialogue between the religions without accurate knowledge of one another."[6]

Same and Other: Must Orthodoxy Be Oppressive?

I will take it for granted that Christian theologians can agree that the other religions should be treated with charity, justice, and respect. But what exactly do these virtues entail? Is it the case that every Christian truth-claim is an assault on the integrity of other religions? Must everyone entertain the same opinion *(ortho-doxa)* as I or receive a violent reprisal? Must orthodoxy be repressive?

Introducing the "Other"

Who is the Other? The Other is that which is not "us" — "them." In the Christian West, this meant that the Other was until the sixteenth century "pagan"; during the Age of Reason "unenlightened"; in the nineteenth century, "primitive"; in the twentieth century, "different."[7] In our times, then, the Other is first and foremost a hermeneutical problem, an often intractable interpretive challenge that resists our faltering attempts to understand it.

Emmanuel Lévinas accuses Western philosophy of a totalizing and

5. Cited in William C. Placher, *Unapologetic Theology: A Christian Voice in a Pluralistic Conversation* (Louisville: Westminster/John Knox Press, 1989), p. 15.

6. Hans Küng, "Christianity and World Religions: Dialogue with Islam," in Leonard Swidler, ed., *Toward a Universal Theology of Religion* (Maryknoll, NY: Orbis, 1987), p. 194.

7. I am here following Bernard McGrane's typology as explored in *Beyond Anthropology: Society and the Other* (New York: Columbia University Press, 1989).

totalitarian discourse. Thought is nothing less than the violence by which the Other is reduced to the Same; knowledge of others becomes knowledge of oneself. "Greek" represents the language and rule of the concept, the universal.[8] In "Greek" thinking, the Other is subdued, captured by consciousness; difference is domesticated. Philosophy tries to reduce the Many to the One, the Other to the Same. Because "identity" is defined in opposition to "difference," the task of philosophy is to overcome otherness. So construed, philosophy is the report of a conquest, not a genuine encounter.

For Lévinas, it is the face of the Other that ultimately eludes philosophy's grasp.[9] The Other's face proclaims a difference between the other and myself that cannot be dissolved: "I cannot make him mine, nor reduce him to my cognition of him."[10] In place of totality is plurality, which abandons the logic of assimilating members to classes. The face of the Other is an infinite end in itself.[11] Our capacity for grasping reality is exceeded by my infinite duty to the Other: to protect the Other's otherness becomes the prime ethical imperative, and perhaps a description of what it is to love.[12]

Theology and the Other

That there is an Other that cannot simply be assimilated by me presents a challenge that is both epistemological and ethical. How have systematic theologians responded? Pluralists level two charges against theologians who have not yet crossed the Rubicon. First, the soteriological critique: Christian theology is exclusivistic. Wilfred Cantwell Smith expresses outrage at the narrow-minded mentality of theologians of the narrow road: "It is morally not possible actually to go out into the world and say to devout, intelligent, fellow human beings: 'We are saved and you are damned.'"[13] Second, the epistemological critique: Christian theology is repressive. Interestingly, this critique is directed against the inclusivist as often as the exclusivist. Both

8. See Robert Gibbs, *Correlations in Rosenzweig and Lévinas* (Princeton, NJ: Princeton University Press, 1992), ch. 7.

9. See E. Lévinas, "Ethics as First Philosophy," in Seán Hand, ed., *The Lévinas Reader* (Oxford: Basil Blackwell, 1989), pp. 75-87.

10. Gibbs, p. 165.

11. Cf. Gibbs, p. 159: "For Lévinas, the ethical obligates me in the face of an other; my objection against the universal is not ultimately for my own sake as the unique individual, but is for the sake of the other person, whose individuality is lost."

12. Cf. Gibbs, p. 184: "Love binds me and creates a responsibility for the beloved that has no limits."

13. Cited in Placher, p. 16.

John Hick and George Lindbeck claim, for instance, that Rahner's notion of the "anonymous Christian" is as imperialistic and deeply offensive to non-Christians as exclusivism.[14] The inclusivist too forces the Other into a category that the Other does not acknowledge. Küng, pertinently, asks whether Christians would be happy to be termed "anonymous Muslims."[15]

There seem to be, then, two strategies that Christian theologians may adopt vis-à-vis the Other: conversion or conversation. Conversion, by remaking the other into the same, does to the other in practice what "Greek" thinking does to the other in theory. David Tracy speaks for pluralists who opt for the second strategy: "I believe that we are fast approaching the day when it will not be possible to attempt a Christian systematic theology except in serious conversation with the other great ways."[16] Theology needs to encompass within its horizons the religious experience of all humanity. Wilfred Cantwell Smith is another who claims that theology is inseparable from the history of religions: "From now on any serious intellectual statement of the Christian faith must include . . . some sort of doctrine of other religions. We explain the fact that the Milky Way is there by the doctrine of creation, but how do we explain that the Bhagavad Gita is there?"[17] Pluralists such as Panikkar think that Christian theologians would do well to converse with Eastern sources now that "Greek" thinking has been exposed as a parched river bed. What the Fathers did with Greek philosophy may point the way forward for theology today. John Cobb claims that the dialogical relation with the religions of Asia today represents "a similar opportunity for reconceptualization in and through engagement with Eastern wisdom."[18]

"Angling": The Nature of Dialogue

The pluralist challenge to the systematic theologian is thus to enter into dialogue in good faith with the Other, with the other religions. Why dia-

14. So Gavin D'Costa, "Theology of Religions," in David F. Ford, ed., *The Modern Theologians,* vol. 2 (Oxford: Basil Blackwell, 1989), p. 282 n. 28.

15. Küng, "Christianity and World Religions," p. 203.

16. David Tracy, *Dialogue with the Other: The Inter-religious Dialogue,* Louvain Theological & Pastoral Monographs (Grand Rapids: Eerdmans, 1991), p. xi.

17. "The Christian in a Religiously Plural World," in J. Hick and B. Hebblethwaite, eds., *Christianity and Other Religions* (London: Collins, 1980), p. 100.

18. John B. Cobb, Jr., "The Religions," in Peter C. Hodgson and Robert H. King, eds., *Christian Theology: An Introduction to Its Traditions and Tasks* (Philadelphia: Fortress, 1985), p. 371.

logue? Küng's response is a model of conciseness: "'War.' I believe that this is indeed the alternative to religious dialogue."[19] Assuming for the moment that this is sufficient reason to enter into conversation with the Other, we then need to inquire into the nature and implications of dialogue.

Dialogue as Wager and Commitment

To what do we commit ourselves when we enter into interreligious dialogue? Minimally, to the formal criteria implicit in rational conversation, namely, the willingness to validate what one proposes and the absence of constraints on what the Other can say in response. Jürgen Moltmann states that in serious dialogue "there can be no valid evasion of difficult questions by recourse to a higher authority not open to critical inspection by others."[20] Moreover, to enter into a dialogue then implies the possibility that one will not emerge unchanged. Indeed, the full cost of dialogue is only here exposed: we must be prepared to put our most cherished beliefs at stake. James DiNoia applies the Golden Rule to interreligious dialogue: do unto Others as you would have them do unto you.

But in order to do justice to the Other, must we also follow the pluralists in their assumption that interreligious dialogue presupposes a commonality of subject matter? To enter into conversation in true pluralist spirit, must one check all one's commitments at the door? The pluralist assumption that dialogue is a means to truth depends on the presupposition that all religions are really expressions of the same fundamental reality. But *is* the Other best served by the pluralist presupposition that the various religions are all talking about the same thing?

The Angler as Paradigm for a Nonpluralistic Dialogue

Against the pluralists, I wish to take Izaak Walton's description of the "Compleat Angler" as an alternative paradigm for engaging the Other. The opening chapters of *The Compleat Angler* consist of a dialogue between a fisherman, a hunter, and a falconer concerning the relative merits of their three sports. Walton's work brings to mind another dialogue about religious pluralism: Lessing's *Nathan the Wise*. Walton himself belonged to a group

19. Küng, "Christianity and World Religions," p. 194.
20. Jürgen Moltmann, "Is 'Pluralistic Theology' Useful for the Dialogue of World Religions," in Gavin D'Costa, ed., *The Myth of Christian Uniqueness Reconsidered: The Myth of a Pluralistic Theory of Religions* (Maryknoll, NY: Orbis, 1990), p. 153.

of intellectuals, called the Great Tew, who believed in religious moderation. As has been noted, Anglers are an obvious metaphor in Walton's book for Anglicans.[21]

The Angler has commitments, but he is willing to be tolerant of others and to argue his case with humility and humor as well as conviction, as the following quotation attests: "Angling is much more ancient than the Incarnation of our Saviour; for in the Prophet *Amos* mention is made of *fish-hooks* . . ." (p. 23). Walton also offers the reader a short contemplation of rivers. Sitting by the River's side, we are told, is the fittest place for Contemplation (p. 24). And, on the debate over whether contemplation or action be the happiness of humanity in the world, Walton argues that both meet together in the art of Angling (p. 24). "Angling" — with its overtones of trying for, gaining a perspective on — stands for the contemplative attitude of one who stands on the shores of the theological Rubicon and sits on the banks of the Ganges.

On the "Identity" of God

In what follows I want to relocate the problem of religious pluralism from soteriology to theology proper. I will examine the three options — exclusivism, inclusivism, pluralism — with regard to the question "Are the other religions concerned with the same reality as is the Christian faith?" Crossing the theological Rubicon into a pluralistic theology of religions means taking a position on the "identity" of God. "Identity" is, of course, susceptible of several meanings: numeric oneness, ontological sameness or permanence in time, and the personal identity of self-continuity.

Two Kinds of Identity

I wish to contrast two kinds of identity, to which I shall refer, following Paul Ricoeur, by the Latin terms *idem* (= sameness) and *ipse* (= selfhood).[22] I will superimpose Ricoeur's distinction upon one drawn by Robert Jenson between two kinds of God. This juxtaposition is not arbitrary, for both

21. So Jonquil Bevan, "Introduction" to Izaak Walton, *The Compleat Angler* (London: J. M. Dent, 1993), p. xviii. The following references are to this edition.

22. Paul Ricoeur, *Oneself as Another,* tr. Kathleen Blarney (Chicago: University of Chicago, 1992).

Ricoeur and Jenson are concerned with the question of identity through, or over, time. Jenson distinguishes two kinds of God by the different ways in which each construes eternity. Every eternity, as a union of past and future, will be one of two broad kinds: a "Persistence of the Beginning" kind or an "Anticipation of the End" kind, for religion is either an attempt to escape from or a trust in the ultimate meaningfulness of temporality.[23]

Idem Identity and the Philosopher's God

What Jenson calls the Persistence of the Beginning kind of God I shall call the God of *idem*-identity, identity under the sign of the Same. The God of *idem*-identity is the philosophers' God and is identified by uncovering the properties of "perfect being." This "Hellenic" interpretation of God posits a timeless ground of Being above the temporal flux: an Unmoved Mover. This supreme Substance became the immutable God of classical theism. In Aristotle and the tradition of classical logic, identity is sameness, which is exclusive of otherness. The "Hellenic" interpretation of Being as an eternal self-same unity thus leads to a monistic ontology. Every differentiation must, on this view, be regarded as a tendency toward nonbeing. As we have seen, Lévinas reads the history of Western thought precisely as the pursuit of identity, that is, as the process of excluding difference and of reducing the Other to the Same. Augustine, in Jenson's opinion, relates the three persons of the Trinity to the divine substance not only equally, but *identically*, so that the differences between the persons are irrelevant to the being of God.[24] Accordingly, "The inheritance of Hellenic interpretation was received as what the scholastics would come to call 'natural' theology, a supposed body of truth about [the one] God shared with the heathens" (p. 117).

Ipse Identity and the God of Abraham, Isaac, and Jacob

Jenson's Anticipation of the End kind of God bears a striking similarity to what Ricoeur calls *ipse*-identity in his discussion of personal identity, the identity of self-constancy rather than sameness. God identifies himself

---

23. Robert W. Jenson, *The Triune Identity: God According to the Gospel* (Philadelphia: Fortress, 1982).

24. "When the Nicenes call the Trinity as such God, they so named him *because* of the triune relations and differences; when Augustine calls the Trinity as such God, it is *in spite* of them" (p. 119).

to Israel as Yahweh and ties his proper name to a promise. It follows that the identity of God is tied up with his power to do what he says rather than with the sameness of substance. The "Hebrew" interpretation of God sees God not as standing apart from time but as standing faithful *through* it. God is true not because God lies unperturbed outside time but because God can be relied upon in time, and until the end of time. In Jenson's words: "The continuity of his being is not that of a defined entity, some of whose defining characteristics persist from beginning to end. It is rather the sort of continuity we have come to call 'personal'; it is established in his words and commitments, by the faithfulness of his later acts to the promises made in his earlier acts" (p. 40).

Ipse-identity — selfhood — is not merely sameness. To be a self is to do more than enjoy an uninterrupted persistence in time. And yet, to be a self, there must be some principle of permanence through time.[25] But is there a kind of permanence in time that is not simply the continuity of the Same? It is here that Jenson's account can be bolstered by Ricoeur's theory of narrative identity, which relates the search for a principle of permanence in time to the question "Who?" rather than "What?"[26] The principle in question is that of keeping one's word. The continuity of the Same is one thing, the constancy of friendship or a promise quite another. *Ipse*-identity, centered on the self's constancy to its word, does not exclude otherness, but requires it.

Identifying "God"

Pluralists argue for dialogue, for an encounter with the alterity of the Other rather than a reduction of the Other to Self. Ironically, however, most theologians who have crossed the Rubicon reduce the particularities and otherness of the gospel's narrative identification of God to a bland, homo-

---

25. For a philosophical discussion of the problem of self-continuity, see Terence Penelhum, "Personal Identity," in *The Encylopedia of Philosophy*, vol. 6 (London: Collier Macmillan, 1967), pp. 95-107.

26. Ricoeur acknowledges an aspect of sameness in personal identity too: character. Character pertains to those aspects of my existence that I am unable to change or, as Ricoeur puts it, "Character is truly the 'what' of the 'who'" (p. 122). It is important to note that the stories of God's acts do not make him what he is, but reveal him for what he has been from all eternity and always will be. The narrative does not constitute God's being, but reveals it. I am arguing, however, that the narratives are a necessary mediation: ontological reflection alone does not allow us to identify the Christian God over against the others.

geneous, unitive or "monistic" pluralism in which the differences in the Christian identification of God are subsumed, sometimes violently, under the intolerant category of the Same.

On Referring to God

Are the various religions referring to the same God? Pannenberg argues that Christianity must presuppose a general idea of God as identifying the subject to which it ascribes various attributes on the basis of God's actions. In Scripture, a general idea of God *('elohim)* underlies the statement that Yahweh alone is God (Isa. 43:10-11). The content of this general idea seems to be the God of the philosophers, namely, the eternal, infinite one who is the origin of the cosmos. For Pannenberg, this is the minimal condition presupposed in all religious talk about God. However, Pannenberg goes on to assert that this minimal concept of God "is not identical with the essence of God which reveals itself in his historical acts."[27] Only in his further revelation does God show us "what it means to be God" (p. 394).

An entity may be identified by means of definite descriptions or by proper names (and titles). A definite description designates a specific individual by creating a class that has but a single member (e.g., first, man, walk, moon). Proper names designate an individual as well, but without giving any information about it (e.g., Neil Armstrong). Jenson states: "The doctrine of the Trinity comprises both a proper name, 'Father, Son and Holy Spirit' . . . and an elaborate development and analysis of corresponding identifying descriptions."[28] There are certain central identifying descriptions of God in the Scriptures: in the Old Testament, God is known as "the one who brought Israel out of Egypt" (Deut. 5:6); in the New Testament, as "the one who raised Jesus from the dead" (Rom. 4:24).

Those who have crossed the Rubicon into a pluralistic theology of religion have usually done so on the basis of a different account of religious reference. The problem with identifying by definite description, they say, is that such descriptions inevitably grow into doctrines. And, as world history has shown, doctrinal descriptions divide. If reference is secured by an accurate doctrinal description, it follows that most accounts of God would be false. Maurice Wiles proposes, as an alternative to doctrinal description, a "causal

---

27. Wolfhart Pannenberg, *Systematic Theology,* vol. 1, tr. Geoffrey W. Bromiley (Grand Rapids: Eerdmans, 1991), p. 394.

28. Jenson, p. 4. Cf. Exod. 20:2 — the name of God and the narration of his works belong together.

theory" of reference, "in which reference is secured not by a correct definition of the object in question but by the causal-historical relations which link the speaker with the intended referent."[29] What fixes reference to God according to the causal theory is the religious experience of a few mystics or saints. The experience is associated with certain soteriological effects: changed behavior and transformed character. Others who have not had this anchoring experience may nevertheless "borrow" the reference from previous speakers. Proponents of the causal theory argue that identifying descriptions are attempts to define more precisely what is already being referred to as "God." Thus one need not conclude from the fact that people are saying different things about "God" that they are referring to different "gods": "God of the Hebrews, God of the Arabs, God of the Hindus . . . could all be different names for the same being *even if there is no significant overlap in belief about His nature.*"[30]

On the Idea of God as Love

Descriptivists like John Searle, however, find it implausible "to suppose that in the chains of communication, when they do occur, the only intentionality which secures reference is that each speaker intends to refer to the same object as the previous speaker."[31] If this were the case, speakers could use names but they would know nothing of the type of thing named by the name. It is difficult, for instance, to see how the pluralist who relies on the causal theory of reference can say "God is love." If there is not some minimal descriptive content associated with the word "God," how can we know whether we are referring to the power of the whole rather than to an ephemeral feeling? Jenson writes: "Only when we specify *who* or *which* allegedly is God is 'God is' a threat or a promise, a solution or a conundrum."[32]

---

29. Maurice Wiles, *Christian Theology and Inter-religious Dialogue* (London: SCM, 1992), p. 39.

30. Richard B. Miller, "The Reference of 'God,'" *Faith and Philosophy* 3 (1986): 14. Searle in *Intentionality* (see note 31 below) argues that speakers refer, and thus that reference is only successful if the intentional content corresponds to the referent. For Searle, what counts is an intentional description associated with a name (cf. William Alston, "Referring to God" in his *Divine Nature and Human Language* [Ithaca: Cornell University Press, 1989], pp. 103-17). The debate between descriptivist and causal theories of reference is highly technical. For a statement of the causal theory, see Saul Kripke, *Naming and Necessity* (Cambridge, MA: Harvard University Press, 1972), and for a defense of the descriptivist theory see Searle, esp. chs. 8 and 9).

31. John Searle, *Intentionality: An Essay in the Philosophy of Mind* (Cambridge: Cambridge University Press, 1983), p. 249.

32. Jenson, p. xi.

"Love," according to George Lindbeck, loses all meaning apart from a specific context: "The significant things are the distinctive patterns of story, belief, ritual, and behavior that give 'love' and 'God' their specific and sometimes contradictory meanings."[33] Perhaps the God of Buddhists and Hindus loves the world too, but only the Christian identifies God as the one who died on humanity's behalf. A narrative identification of God, on the other hand, can both give "love" content and ascribe love to God. The doctrine of the Trinity is the result of a narrative identification of the Christian God.[34] The Gospels "figure" God — by ascribing certain acts and a pattern of activity — as economic Trinity, as one who relates to the world through Spirit and Son. The ontological Trinity — the belief in the eternality of the triune God — is a "configuration" of this economic figuration. Debates about religious pluralism get bogged down because they start from the *idem*-identity of the *one* God, that is, with an assumption of *sameness*. In a pluralistic theology of religions, God is identified ontologically, by extrapolating from religious experience or through philosophical reflection; the various "economic" relations are considered incidental to the *one* God rather than constitutive revelations of the divine identity. The Fathers, however, identified the one God with the plurality of Father, Son, and Spirit. They thought of God equally in terms of oneness and threeness, and they did so by allowing the narrative to clarify and correct the philosophical identification of God.

The "Theology of Religions"

Early modern philosophers of religion suggested that true religion is natural and rational, available to all. For philosophers such as Kant, particularities that distinguish the ecclesiastical religions are merely secondary features — accidents of history — and thus inessential. Does twentieth-century theology of religions do better in preserving differences and in negotiating the scandal of particularity? Though Christian theologians have always held "doctrines" about other religions (i.e., that other religions teach some truth, that other religions are false, that other religions are fulfilled by Chris-

33. George A. Lindbeck, *The Nature of Doctrine: Religion and Theology in a Postliberal Age* (Philadelphia: Westminster Press, 1984), p. 42.
34. By emphasizing narrative I do not wish to exclude the normative function of other types of biblical literature in identifying God. But narrative adds a specificity to notions such as "love," "power," etc. that these attributes might otherwise lack without a concrete narrative depiction.

tianity), it is only relatively recently, with the demise of rational religion, that a "theology" of religions has been attempted.[35]

Pluralistic Theology of Religions

Briefly stated, a pluralistic theology of religions aims at recognizing the validity of other religions without abandoning Christian faith. Religious pluralists believe that all religions ultimately point to the same truth. Hick's pluralistic hypothesis takes its cue from Kant: the religions are culture-relative ways of experiencing the Real. "According to the pluralistic hypothesis, when we speak of God as known within a particular religious tradition — Jahweh or Adonai, the heavenly Father or the Holy Trinity, Allah, Shiva, Vishnu and so on — we are speaking of a humanly experienced *persona* of the Real."[36] Revelation — the Real as we apprehend it — is always phenomenal; the Real *an sich* is, however, beyond human experience and categories. Otherwise, we would have "either to regard all the reported experiences as illusory or else return to the confessional position in which we affirm the authenticity of our own stream of religious experience whilst dismissing as illusory those occurring within other traditions" (p. 249). Neither of these options, however, strikes Hick as "realistic." Why not?

The pluralist begins the interreligious dialogue with a conviction of sorts about the "rough parity" between the religions. To enter into true dialogue with the Other means, for the pluralist, recognizing that there is some sort of truth in the Other.[37] According to the pluralist, inclusivists are just as monistic as exclusivists when it comes to religious truth claims (i.e., concerning the finality of Jesus as Savior) — they simply wish to affirm that more people are saved on their view than under an exclusivist soteriological scheme.

---

35. See DiNoia, *The Diversity of Religions* (Washington, DC: Catholic University of America Press, 1992), ch. 1. On the development of history and theology of religions see Paul Knitter, *Toward a Protestant Theology of Religions: A Case Study of Paul Althaus and Contemporary Attitudes* (1974) and Heinz Schlette, *Towards a Theology of Religions* (New York: Herder and Herder, 1966). This book pertains to salvation history in particular. See Pannenberg for the theology of the history of religions.

36. John Hick, *An Interpretation of Religion: Human Responses to the Transcendent* (London: Macmillan, 1989), p. 258. Hick rightly sees his pluralistic hypothesis as espousing a modalistic construal of the Trinity (pp. 271-72).

37. Langdon B. Gilkey, "The Pluralism of Religions," in Arvind Sharma, ed., *God, Truth and Reality: Essays in Honour of John Hick* (New York: St. Martin's Press, 1993), p. 111.

A "World" Theology of Religions

Whereas Hick see all religions as paths to the same truth, Gordon Kaufman believes that truth emerges only in the course of conversation: "I call this a 'pluralistic' or 'dialogical' conception of truth."[38] But surely Kaufman here is confusing the concept of truth with the manner in which we attain it. In the end or, better, *at* the end, truth is still one for the pluralist. All religions are equally valid ways to the same truth. It thus comes as no surprise that many pluralists now openly advocate a "world" or "universal" theology of religions. Wilfred Cantwell Smith argues that a theology of religions is "universal" if it draws its data from all religions. And in N. Ross Reat and Edmund F. Perry's *A World Theology,* the monistic tendency of pluralistic theologies of religions is made explicit. Their thesis is both clear and simple: the world religions are different expressions of the same central spiritual reality of humanity — "God." As the central spiritual reality of humanity, "God" is "an expression of the human necessity of affirming meaning and purpose in one's life as a whole."[39] "God" is thus undeniable and desirable. "God" is also, as all the religions acknowledge, ultimately elusive.

This last dimension — elusiveness — is vital for world theology, as the authors point out: "Each religion thus embraces in its very heart a paradox. On the one hand, each disclaims that it totally comprehends ultimate reality. On the other hand, each claims to have supreme access, understanding, and relation to ultimate reality. This paradox signifies more than any religion has discerned, or has admitted responsibly" (p. 22). In spite of their case for a world theology, Reat and Perry claim that they do not intend "to encourage the sacrifice of particularity on the altar of universality" (p. 311). As symbolic expressions of the same central spiritual reality, the several religions may be mutually complementary rather than mutually exclusive of one another (p. 23).

Can the Trinity fit into such a schema? Interestingly, though the authors rightly recognize the Christian belief that Jesus' person and work reveals God, they claim that Christianity's "theocentricity" entails that "even the revelation of God in Christ [is] itself relative to God whose reality exceeds all that is revealed in Christ" (p. 206). The Christian claim that Jesus is the only way and truth "contradicts the Christian theocentric axiom that God alone is absolute" (p. 207). The doctrine of the Trinity sits uneasily in such a scheme, particu-

---

38. Gordon Kaufman, "Religious Diversity and Religious Truth," in Sharma, ed., p. 158.
39. N. Ross Reat and Edmund F. Perry, *A World Theology: The Central Spiritual Reality of Humankind* (Cambridge: Cambridge University Press, 1991), p. 9.

larly when we learn that God's "personhood" is not a universally attested characteristic of humanity's central spiritual reality.[40]

Against Pluralistic and Universal Theology of Religions

Is a pluralistic or world theology of religions any less exclusivistic and repressive of the "Other" than is orthodox theology? No, and this for several reasons.

Pluralistic Theology of Religions Is Exclusivistic

Does world theology embrace or efface the religiously particular and the different? A number of critics argue that pluralism has by no means escaped an exclusivistic attitude, but merely transposed it from Christianity to modern Western liberalism. According to Gordon D. Kaufman, Hick's position is "utterly monolithic" insofar as it explains that, as far as religious truth claims are concerned, "they all come down to *essentially the same thing.*"[41] Several critics have decried pluralism's illegitimate treatment of religion as a genus.[42] To the extent that the pluralist defines the core of religion, then, the very concept of religion must be exclusivistic: some phenomena will be in, others out. For example, Küng is quite sure that "one cannot place magic or belief in witches, alchemy, or the like, on the same level with belief in the existence of God. . . ."[43] But why can we not? Because such phenomena do not correspond to the contemporary liberal intellectual tradition to which most pluralists belong.[44]

---

40. I discovered only one brief reference to the Trinity in the authors' sixty-six-page chapter on Christianity.

41. Kaufman, p. 162 n. 2.

42. See John Milbank, "The End of Dialogue," in D'Costa, ed., *Christian Uniqueness Reconsidered*, pp. 174-91; Alister E. McGrath, "The Christian Church's Response to Pluralism," *Journal of the Evangelical Theological Society* 35 (1992): 487-501; and especially Robert T. Osborne, "From Theology to Religion," *Modern Theology* 8 (1992): 75-88.

43. Küng, "What Is True Religion? Toward an Ecumenical Criteriology," in Swidler, p. 236.

44. See John V. Apczynski, "John Hick's Theocentrism: Revolutionary or Implicitly Exclusivistic?" *Modern Theology* 8 (1992): 39-52. Roger T. Osborn argues that the idea of "religion" itself is repressive, in that it was originally a projection of Christianity onto other phenomena. It then became possible to look at Christianity as the best exemplification of "true religion." See Roger T. Osborn, "From Theology to Religion," *Modern Theology* 8 (1992): 75-88.

Pluralistic Theology of Religions Is Repressive

Not only does a pluralistic theology of religions keep some phenomena out, but those that are let in must conform to the prevailing interpretive framework. D'Costa charges pluralism with itself being imperialistic and absolutist inasmuch as it proposes "to incorporate religions on the system's own terms rather than on terms in keeping with the self-understanding of the religions."[45] Kathryn Tanner observes that pluralism is a form of colonialist discourse that hinders rather than helps interreligious dialogue: "In imitation of the general way colonialist discourse constructs its 'Others,' the pluralist insistence on identity in beliefs, norms, or reference as a presupposition for inter-religious dialogue undermines, I argue, respect for other religions *as other.*"[46]

Pluralistic Theology of Religions Is "Interested"

Is pluralistic theology a theology without a concrete religious practice to support it, or is it the expression of a new religious faith? Pannenberg worries that Smith begins his theology of religions with a knowledge of God that is independent of the religious traditions. But where would such a knowledge come from? Paul Knitter and other pluralists wield a liberationist-pragmatic criterion for "true" religion: the concern for human welfare, not doctrine, provides a ground both for religious cooperation and for criticism of religion. But this stance is every bit as ideological as an exclusivistic theology of religions.

Hans Küng proposes the "humanum" as a general ethical criterion with which one can judge the truth of a religion. True religion, he says, may not commend "what appears to be inhuman. . . ."[47] Appears to whom? I would not be at all surprised if celibacy did not appear as inhumane as cannibalism to some of the "humane modernists" whom Küng has in mind. Though Küng rightly recognizes that the fundamental question is "What is good for human beings?" he fails to see the inadequacy of his answer: "What helps them to be truly human" (p. 242). Is not the nature, meaning, and goal of the humanum precisely what is disputed in the religions?

Küng, of course, has his own vision of the humanum: "whatever clearly

45. Gavin D'Costa, "Introduction," in D'Costa, ed., *Christian Uniqueness Reconsidered,* p. ix.

46. Kathryn Tanner, "Respect for Other Religions: A Christian Antidote to Colonialist Discourse," *Modern Theology* 9 (1993): 1.

47. Küng, "What Is True Religion?" p. 240.

protects, heals, and fulfills human beings in their physico-psychic, individual-social humanity" (p. 242). But, as Paul Eddy points out, it is hard to see Küng's liberationist criterion as anything other than an arbitrary preference. Either one truly does abandon any "interested" viewpoint and accepts all notions at the dialogue table, "or else one acknowledges *some* meta-criteriological touch-stone by which the various dialogical viewpoints are to be evaluated."[48]

Pluralistic Theology of Religions Is Bland

Perhaps the blandness of a pluralistic theology of religion is its worst fault — religion should never be boring! And yet Hick manages to reduce the rich tapestry of religious belief and practice to a throw rug (all synthetic, with no natural fibers). Hick discounts the significance of doctrine; religious truth is not cognitive so much as transformative. What it is that transforms us is, however, very difficult to specify. DiNoia complains that pluralists tend "to homogenize cross-religious variations in doctrines of salvation in the direction of an indeterminate common goal."[49] Kenneth Surin similarly calls attention to the inevitable result — differences become *merely* cultural: "monological pluralism sedately but ruthlessly domesticates and assimilates the other — *any* other — in the name of world ecumenism."[50]

A Trinitarian Theology of Religions?

It is surprising that the Trinity, with its unique solution to the problem of the one and the many, is not more regularly invoked in the theology of religions.[51] The present essay tries to remedy this lacuna. My intent is to bring the resources of trinitarian theology to bear on the question of religious pluralism in a more direct manner by focusing on the question of the identity of "God" rather than on soteriology.[52]

48. Paul R. Eddy, "Paul Knitter's Theology of Religions: A Survey and Evangelical Response," *Evangelical Quarterly* 65 (1993): 243.

49. DiNoia, p. 48.

50. Kenneth Surin, "A 'Politics of Speech': Religious Pluralism in the Age of McDonald's Hamburger," in D'Costa, ed., *Christian Uniqueness Reconsidered*, p. 200.

51. D'Costa notes that the Trinity "is very rarely mentioned in Christian theologies of religion." D'Costa, "Theology of Religions," p. 287.

52. David Burrell, in his review of *Christian Uniqueness Reconsidered*, says that its first two chapters confirm one's suspicions "that a deeper Christian appropriation of our trinitarian faith will open such [interreligious] conversations in an illuminating manner" (*Modern Theology* 9 [1993]: 309).

Raimundo Panikkar: The "Perichoresis" of Religions

Panikkar is the exception that proves the rule, a pluralist who *does* invoke the Trinity and who believes it to be at the heart of all human religions.[53] Panikkar criticizes "unitive" pluralism for some of the same reasons that we have already rehearsed, most notably for its presumption that a rational universal theory of religion is desirable. The Western search for a universal theory (monologue) is only one way of expressing human religiosity. True pluralism (dialogue) is a matter of mutually exclusive ultimate systems, which cannot, by definition, be grounded in a common denominator or resolved in a higher synthesis. Truth itself is pluralistic, by which Panikkar means that there is no one absolute truth.

Panikkar believes that Eastern thought, particularly the nondualist or advaitist tradition of Hinduism, is more congruent with Christian trinitarian thought than the dualist philosophy of the ancient Greeks. "Christianness" (symbolized by the Ganges) refers to the mystical core of religion rather than its institutional or doctrinal forms. Panikkar wishes to make a suprarational "cosmic confidence in reality," rather than a universal theory of religions, the basis for interreligious conversation and cooperation. Each concrete religion offers only a perspective, a window to the whole. It is vital that we are aware that we see the whole through a part, for only then can we concede that the Other may also have a view of the whole. The very incommensurability of the religions is the condition for a kind of trinitarian perichoresis in which each religion is a dimension of the other, since each represents the whole of the human experience in a concrete way. Both the Other and I see the whole, but only under one particular aspect: "Christianity has no proper name for the Supreme Being. 'God' is a common name. . . . All this suggests the possibility of a Christianness different from Christendom and Christianity. . . . 'Christ' is the symbol for the divine-human mystery 'which is at work everywhere and elusively present wherever there is reality.' "[54] Against the monism of exclusivism, inclusivism, and unitive pluralism alike, Panikkar proposes a view of Reality as radically free

---

53. Raimundo Panikkar, *The Trinity and the Religious Experience of Man: Icon-Person-Mystery* (Maryknoll, NY: Orbis and London: Darton, Longman & Todd, 1973), p. viii. Rowan Williams judges Pannikar's book on the Trinity to be "one of the best and least read meditations on the Trinity in our century" ("Trinity and Pluralism," in D'Costa, ed., *Christian Uniqueness Reconsidered*, p. 3).

54. Panikkar, "The Jordan, the Tiber, and the Ganges," pp. 106, 113. Or, as Demarest paraphrases: "Christ is the non-historic Logos, confessed by Christians as Jesus but known in other religions by different names" (p. 221).

(i.e., free from being assimilated by thought). And yet reality can be trusted because it is ordered, though the order is more like the harmony of music than the hierarchy of a system: "Concord is neither oneness nor plurality. It is the dynamism of the Many toward the One without ceasing to be different and without becoming one, and without reaching a higher synthesis. . . . There is no harmonical accord if there is no plurality of sounds, or if those sounds coalesce in one single note."[55]

The Christian symbol of this harmony is, for Panikkar, the Trinity. The Father stands for the nameless Absolute. The Son is the divine Person in whom humans participate. The Spirit is the principle of unity in which the nameless Absolute and named persons participate. The Trinity is thus a symbol for "theandrism" — "that intimate and complete unity . . . between the divine and the human . . . which is the goal towards which everything here below tends."[56] Reality is "theandric"; each being is a christophany, an intrinsic part of the whole. There are neither two realities (God and man) nor one (God or man). This is the central message of the Upanishads — "God is in all; all is in God" — that cannot be communicated in words or concepts. We know God immediately in the depths of spiritual experience.

Western theology has lost this sense of cosmic harmony through its overemphasis on the Logos (thought/consciousness) over against a true plurality of truths (Spirit as freedom). "What I am against ultimately is the total dominion of the *logos* and a subordinationism of the Spirit — to put it in Christian trinitarian words — or against any form of monism, in philosophical parlance."[57] Panikkar adopts a nondualistic, advaitic attitude that holds that reality is itself pluralistic: "Being as such, even if 'encompassed' by or 'co-existent' with the Logos or a Supreme Intelligence, does not need to be reduced to consciousness."[58] By denying the equivalence of Being and Consciousness, Panikkar represents one possible response to Lévinas's injunction to let the Other "be" rather than assimilating it to thought. Indeed, Panikkar says that if the Logos is the transparency of Being, the Spirit is its opaqueness. Even God has an opacity that resists total intelligibility: "This is precisely the locus of freedom — and the basis of pluralism."[59]

55. Raimundo Panikkar, "The Invisible Harmony: A Universal Theory of Religion or a Cosmic Confidence in Reality?" in Swidler, ed., p. 145.

56. Panikkar, *Trinity and Religious Experience*, p. 71.

57. Panikkar, "Invisible Harmony," p. 124.

58. Panikkar, "The Jordan, the Tiber, and the Ganges," p. 109.

59. Panikkar, "Invisible Harmony," p. 130.

Geist or Gestalt: Configuring Shapes of the Spirit

A number of recent works on the general topic of theology and religious pluralism have followed Panikkar's lead in dealing with the "loyalty-openness" dilemma, that is, the problem of how to be faithful to one's own religion while engaging the Other in dialogue. Though they claim to be trinitarian, each is careful to maintain a certain critical distance between Christology and pneumatology.

We begin with Rowan Williams's "Trinity and Pluralism," an essay on Panikkar's trinitarian pluralism. The Trinity is there seen as an ever-generative source of form (Logos) and realization (Spirit). "Form," however, is never exhausted nor limited by specific realizations. "Christ" is for Panikkar the name of a specific person *and* of the shape of the potential future of all human beings. But the Spirit is the process by which this form is realized "in a diversity as wide as the diversity of the human race itself."[60] As God the Father is constitutive of the identity of Jesus, so God the Spirit is constitutive (in a different sense) of the process of the Church.[61] Williams appears to agree with Panikkar that the mystery of "Christ" will be realized in forms hitherto unknown in Christianity, forms that we may well discover in our encounter with the other religions.

Like Panikkar, Michael Barnes wants to avoid a unitive pluralism. He offers a way beyond the paradigms of exclusivism, inclusivism, and "monological" pluralism, namely, a "dialogal" pluralism.[62] With Panikkar, Barnes sees the religions not as constituting competing systems but as representing different ways of being human. Each religion shares a unique language and practice through which people cope with change and expiate suffering. Religions are united not on the level of beliefs, but on the (deeper) interpersonal level of human religiosity. Religions understand themselves better through dialoguing with others. And at the root of Barnes's theology of religions lies a spirit-centered theory of the interpenetration (perichoresis) of religions. Interreligious dialogue proceeds on the basis of a common human religiosity, which is the work of the Spirit.

Peter Hodgson, drawing largely upon Hegel, similarly believes that

---

60. Rowan Williams, "Trinity and Pluralism," in D'Costa, ed., *Christian Uniqueness Reconsidered*, p. 8.

61. See Rowan Williams, "Trinity and Ontology," in Kenneth Surin, ed., *Christ, Ethics and Tragedy: Essays in Honour of Donald MacKinnon* (Cambridge: Cambridge University Press, 1989), pp. 71-93.

62. Michael Barnes, *Religions in Conversation: Christian Identity and Christian Pluralism* (London: SPCK, 1989), pp. 172ff.

the divine Geist — or, in his terminology, the divine Gestalt — takes different forms in different times (and religions). Hodgson claims that God is present in history in *many* shapes of freedom. But we here encounter a problem, best stated by Gilkey, that confronts all these attempts to "deregulate" the Spirit from its specific Christian context: within the plurality around us "are forms of the religious that are intolerable . . . because they are demonic."[63] Caste, consumerism, sexism, racism — these represent the "dark side" of religion. Gilkey recognizes the pluralist's dilemma: to resist, one must assert some sort of ultimate value, but to do this is to assert a "worldview," which, at least implicitly, implies that other views of reality are mistaken. The pluralist wants both to relativize the religious *and* to resist the demonic. In theory, the dilemma is insoluble; but in praxis we uncover a "relative absoluteness."[64] Hodgson agrees: "the way beyond absolutism and relativism may be found . . . through engagement in some form of transformative, emancipatory praxis."[65] God is present in history precisely as the plurality of shapes of freedom.

Specifically, God is "the One who loves in freedom." Hodgson gives this Barthian formula a distinctly Hegelian twist. "Spirit" becomes a shorthand term for the process by which God enters into relationship with the world, suffers its alienation, and overcomes ("transfigures") the difference. But how can we tell the difference between the divine and the demonic, between forms of freedom and forms of fascism? Apparently, a form of praxis may be configured as "love in freedom" whenever it manifests the dialectical process of identity, difference, and mediation, represented by the figure of Jesus: "Love entails a union mediated by relationship and hence distinction" (p. 99). Significantly, Hodgson identifies the "world" with the moment of difference (p. 106). It is precisely because the world is not-God that it is a moment in the divine life: "God is the identity of God and not-God, the event that takes place between God and the world" (p. 106).

Does the substitution of "world" for "Son of God" as the second moment in the divine life mean that Hodgson's theology is no longer Christian? He replies that theology has traditionally manifested a "potentially idolatrous fixation" on Jesus (p. 106). He cites a number of reasons why theologians should resist this fixation — not only the conceptual dif-

---

63. Langdon B. Gilkey, "Plurality and Its Theological Implications," in Hick and Knitter, eds., *The Myth of Christian Uniqueness,* p. 44.

64. Gilkey, "Plurality and Its Theological Implications," p. 47.

65. Peter C. Hodgson, *God in History: Shapes of Freedom* (Nashville: Abingdon, 1989), p. 41. The following citations refer to this work.

ficulties of incarnation Christology, but also the sad history of Jewish per-
secution, feminism, and religious pluralism. But, having loosened the ties
that bind us to Jesus, Hodgson nevertheless confidently speaks of "God's
loving, suffering, transformative embrace of the world" (p. 107), which
appears not all at once but in a plurality of forms, of which none can claim
exclusive validity. For Christians, the paradigmatic "shape" by which God's
love for the world is discerned is the life and death of Jesus, whose cross
constitutes the "divine gestalt." But "God" is present in a transfiguring way
in all the many shapes of liberating praxis, not just the Christian: "God
takes shape in other religions as well, and their claims are as legitimate as
ours" (p. 214).

Hodgson's treatment leads one to inquire into the basis of this configuration of God as the "one who loves in freedom." How can we know
that God is love, much less that the same God is at work in all religions,
apart from his self-identification as this (or that) God? After all, the divine
Gestalt can be disfigured as well as configured. And is freedom a gift of the
Heilige Geist or the necessary end point of Hegel's *Geist?* Is the mystery of
love nothing more than the mystery of Hegelian dialectics?

Whose Trinity? What Spirit? Which Pluralism?

What seems to unite pluralistic trinitarian theologies of religion is the role
of the Spirit as a "universalizer." The Spirit resists the reduction of Being
(Father) to Logos (Son); consequently, no one religious "form" can lay claim
to have caught the fullness of reality. D'Costa remarks: "Pneumatology
allows the particularity of Christ to be related to the universal activity of
God in the history of humankind."[66] No friend to pluralism, D'Costa
nevertheless believes (on the basis of passages such as John 16) that divine
revelation is not limited to the particularities of Jesus' history — the Spirit
will guide us into even *more* truth. Because the Spirit "blows where it will,"
the activity of the Spirit cannot be confined to Christianity. The underlying
question that must be asked of these trinitarian theologies of religions
concerns the manner in which, and the extent to which, the Spirit is the
Spirit of Jesus Christ.

Bruce Demarest contends that what Panikkar calls "Spirit" derives
more from speculative philosophy than from Christian theology. He refers

66. D'Costa, "Christ, the Trinity and Religious Plurality," in D'Costa, ed., *Christian Uniqueness Reconsidered*, p. 19.

to Panikkar's adoption of a pantheistic monistic Hindu perspective of humanity's essential identity with transcendent Reality as an "unholy union" of Christian faith and Eastern spirituality.[67] Tempering Demarest's assessment somewhat, we might say that Panikkar has exchanged a Western monism (of reason) for an Eastern one (of Spirit). Panikkar would doubtless wish to distinguish metaphysical monism from his vision of cosmic harmonic unity. But what looks like pluralism may merely be a muddier monism, where everything is a mixture of everything else in a kind of metaphysical perichoresis. Indeed, Timothy Bradshaw has argued that if various religions hold a common trinitarianism, it is only a subordinationist or cosmological kind that seeks to construct a bridge between God and the world.[68]

John Milbank similarly believes that Panikkar's attempt to equate trinitarian and Neo-Vedantic pluralism falls short of orthodox trinitarian theology. Panikkar's nondualist pluralism acknowledges differences as realities to be encountered, but fails to arrive at a valuation of the Other insofar as the transcendent is an "indifferent" presence and power. For Milbank, only in a Christian trinitarianism "can one both fulfill respect for the other and complete and secure this otherness as pure neighborly difference."[69]

D'Costa proposes the following axiom, designed to show that truth criteria in discussions of religious pluralism are always tradition-specific: "in relation to the decreased specificity of an alleged neutral proposal its usefulness diminishes."[70] I believe we can sum up the aforementioned criticisms concerning "pneumatological pluralism" with a similar axiom: "in relation to the decreased specificity of 'Spirit,' its usefulness in a theology of religion diminishes."[71] If the Spirit's activity were literally universal, we would not be able to distinguish the divine from the demonic. Williams

---

67. Demarest, p. 223.

68. Timothy Bradshaw, "The Ontological Trinity," *Scottish Journal of Theology* 29 (1976): 301-10. Bradshaw says that it is another question altogether to ask "whether the 'orthodox' formulation of triunity has parallels of its own in the history of religions" (p. 305).

69. Milbank, "End of Dialogue," p. 188. Williams disagrees, saying that the heart of Panikkar's ontology can be summarized by saying that "differences matter" ("Trinity and Pluralism," p. 4).

70. Gavin D'Costa, "Whose Objectivity? Which Neutrality?" *Religious Studies* 29 (1993): 81.

71. It is noteworthy that, while John the Baptist acknowledged his diminishing role with regard to Jesus — "He must increase, but I must decrease" (John 3:30) — Jesus does not similarly cede his place to the Spirit. On the contrary, Jesus says of the Spirit "He will bear witness of Me" (John 15:26) and "He shall glorify Me" (John 16:14).

seems to concede this point, implicitly invoking the Reformed emphasis on the necessity of both Word and Spirit, when he says that if the Christic principle — what Hodgson calls the divine *"Gestalt"* — is to have the capacity to challenge current versions of "humanity's common good," it must do so "in the name of its own central and *historically* distinctive Trinitarian insight."[72]

"Relating" God: From Narrative to Ontology

The Christian goal in interfaith dialogue is to invite Others into the narrative that "relates" God and identifies God as one who, in his inner and outer trinitarian relations (i.e., in God's being and acts), is love. I offer the following remarks on "relating God" as a contribution to the resolution of the "loyalty-openness" dilemma (i.e., how to hold convictions *and* a conversation). I have argued that pluralistic theologies of religions typically work with an *idem* concept of God's identity, which seeks to do ontology without narrative mediation. I now wish to develop my earlier suggestion that the biblical narrative's identification of God as triune gives rise to an ontology wherein differences are neither reduced nor repressed, but reconciled — "saved."

Narrative Identity: The Triune God

Following Dilthey, Ricoeur notes that narrative articulates personal identity as it is manifested in a life history. The identity of the character "is constructed in connection with that of the plot."[73] Now a "plot" is a way of "configuring" heterogeneous events and persons into a meaningful whole. Narrative (not metaphysics, as in Panikkar) thus mediates between concordance and discordance. The narrative operation has developed "an entirely original concept of dynamic identity which reconciles the same categories that Locke took as contraries: identity and diversity" (p. 143). The identity of the character is so dependent on the narrative operation that Ricoeur claims: "characters . . . are themselves plots" (p. 143).

Each person's life history is "entangled" in the histories of others.

---

72. Williams, "Trinity and Pluralism," p. 10. He also remarks: "Witness to the 'christic fact' as an integrating reality proposes to the world of faiths the possibility of a kind of critical human norm that can be used in the struggle against what limits or crushes humanity" (p. 9).

73. Ricoeur, p. 143. The following references will be taken from this work.

"Self-constancy is for each person that manner of conducting himself or herself so that others can *count on* that person" (p. 165). A narrative identification reveals the self in its difference with respect to the Same (i.e., character, one's permanence in time) and in its dialectic with respect to the Other (i.e., fidelity, one's self-constancy through time).

I will now develop my earlier suggestion that Jenson's "God according to the Gospel" manifests the *ipse* identity of self-constancy rather than the *idem* identity of self-sameness. With regard to the question of divine identity, we may associate the problematic of sameness with God's oneness, and the problematic of *ipseity* or selfhood with God's threeness. If character is plot, we can identify God only on the basis of his acts, configured as a certain kind of whole with an implicit ethical aim. But this is precisely what we have in Scripture. The Old Testament identifies God as the one who has kept his promises to bring Israel out of Egypt and who will keep his promise to restore Israel. The Gospels identify God as the one who raised his Son from the dead and promised to give him a cosmic kingdom. The biblical narratives confer a "dynamic identity" upon God: God's identity is a matter of his self-constancy to his word. God's identity is a function not merely of the aseity of an indeterminate entity, but of the ipseity of a self.[74]

Of course, the narrative identity of God is complicated by the fact that there seem to be three interrelated life stories: those of Father, Son, and Spirit. Here too, however, the differences as well as the relations between the three persons are articulated by narrative. Who God is, and what God is like, is a function of the entangled life histories of Father, Son, and Spirit related in the Gospels. Jenson is critical of formulations that make the differences and relations between the three persons irrelevant to the identity of God. Such attempts are metaphysical interpretations of deity in terms of timelessness (the *idem* identity associated with Persistence of a Past). Rather, it is the narrative figuration of the economic Trinity — that is, the story of the temporal missions of Jesus and the Spirit — that alone configures God's eternity.

Pannenberg criticizes theologians of both West and East for trying to derive the threeness of persons from the concept of God's essential unity, regardless of whether this unity is conceived as a substance (e.g., by Augustine, Aquinas, Protestant Orthodoxy) or as subject (e.g., Hegel,

---

74. This is not meant as a denial of divine aseity. God does not "acquire" an identity as the plot of universal history develops. Rather, the story of God's relations shows who God always was, is, and will be.

Barth). Pannenberg reverses the traditional order: "it is only with the question of the essence and attributes of the trinitarian God that the unity of this God becomes a theme."[75] However, Pannenberg moves beyond the tradition by "expanding the economy," as it were, and considering the trinitarian relations not only in terms of origin or causality, as did the Cappadocians, but rather in light of the total work of Word and Spirit.

What constitutes the identity of Father, Son, and Spirit is not merely the manner of origin (e.g., begetting, breathing) but the sum total of their multifarious relations. If persons are what they are in their relations to one another, it is illegitimate to reduce the richness of these relations to relations of origin alone: "The persons cannot be identical simply with any one relation. Each is a catalyst of many relations."[76] The Father is as dependent on the triumph of the Son as the Son is on his sending by the Father. Pannenberg accepts Rahner's axiom that the immanent Trinity is the economic; God is the same in his eternal essence as he is in his self-revelation in salvation history. God's unity can be determined only by a configuration of the works of Father, Son, and Spirit in salvation history. This configuration is, of necessity, narrative in nature. Ricoeur's insight that "character is plot" is thus another way of saying that God's ontological unity is derived from God's triune self-manifestation in history. The God of religious pluralism may be self-same, but the Triune God of Christian faith has *character*.

If Jesus is indeed the decisive revelation of God, then God can be true to his Word only if the whole of history manifests the same cross-and-resurrection shape. The Spirit is the Spirit of the humiliated and exalted Christ. Whereas Panikkar and other pluralists try to weaken the ties that bind the Spirit to the Son, a reading of the "expanded economy" that takes account of the diverse relations of Father, Son, and Spirit would, I believe, configure the Spirit as the deputy of Christ rather than as an independent itinerant evangelist.

Ontological Reflection: Love and Marriage

The narrative identification of the triune God leads to an ontological reflection whose climax and conclusion is the declaration "God is love." The only reason this identifying description escapes the fate of other vacuous abstractions is that God's love is given a concrete narrative specification:

75. Pannenberg, *Systematic Theology*, p. 299.
76. Pannenberg, *Systematic Theology*, p. 320.

God's being is such that it continues to pour itself out for others, albeit in different ways. The meaning of "God is love," then, is tied to the narrative configuration of God's being as the fellowship of Father, Son, and Spirit.

The narrative of the Trinity is entangled with other life histories as well. The deity of the Father is a function of his keeping both his Word and his world, insofar as he has chosen to love and identify with it. Jesus asks the Father, "Keep them in Thy name" (John 17:11). The triune identity is one that embraces others in a noncoercive way. The well-being of the Other is constitutive of the identity of God, insofar as God has not only spoken to but *become* a Word of promise for others. The being in communion of the triune God is not the *idem* identity of the Persistence of the Past. There are dynamic relations between the three persons, relations not merely of causality but of faithfulness (i.e., keeping, obeying, abiding, glorifying). Just as the Father's identity is at stake in his promise to the Son, so the Son's identity is at stake in his promise to the disciples (e.g., to send the Spirit and to keep them in the Father's name).

Marriage is also a being in communion constituted by a word of promise. In marriage there is a recognition of both sameness (one flesh) and otherness (two distinct persons). "This mystery is great" (Eph. 5:32) — great enough, perhaps, to illustrate the triune identity? What I am hesitantly trying to articulate is an ontology of marriage, a concrete form of love. What constitutes marriage is fidelity to one's vows, to one's word of promise. The gospel narratives that identify God as Father, Son, and Spirit call for and configure an ontological reflection that recognizes the triune life as constituted by *covenantal,* not causal, relations — relations that help us to understand who God is and what love is.

Milbank has recently argued that the only alternative to an ontology of violence, where everything is either reduced to the Same or else constituted by sheer difference and thus related conflictually, is the ontology of peace that emerges from narratives of Jesus (esp. pp. 427-30).[77] I have in this essay argued that the pluralistic theology of religions, beginning as it does with the *idem* identity of the one God, has not escaped the violence that reduces the Many to the Same. In the triune *ipse* identity, on the other hand, peace and harmony are gained not by excluding the Other, but by God's covenant promise to be for the creature *precisely in its difference* from its Creator. Difference — internal and external to the trinitarian life — is the condition for fidelity and fellowship.

77. John Milbank, *Theology and Social Theory* (Oxford: Basil Blackwell, 1990), esp. pp. 427-30.

Relating to Others: The Nature of Dialogue and the Dilemma of "Loyalty-Openness"

True pluralism — the kind that respects the alterity of the other rather than assimilating it — is possible only on trinitarian grounds. This follows from the fact that one's ethics and epistemology are rooted in ontology. The Trinity, then, far from hindering conversation, is the transcendental condition of interfaith dialogue with the Other. Without the Trinity, theological dialogue lacks the necessary specificity (i.e., Logos, Christ) and the necessary spirit (i.e., love, Spirit) to prosper. Our Angler's dialogical dilemma is, at least, clearer: he must be open to differences while at the same time minding distinctives.

Saving the Differences

One may seek in charity to be, as far as is conceptually and confessionally possible, at peace with all positions, but one must then seek, in clarity, to enumerate the differences that remain. DiNoia offers a salient reminder: "recognizing differences is not equivalent to promoting discord. It is a way of taking other people seriously."[78] Recognizing the other in his alterity is thus an ethical imperative for the Christian. Kathryn Tanner appeals to the doctrine of creation as a means of saving the differences: we should respect others because they are God's creatures too. "Identity in fundamental beliefs or ultimate reference is no precondition for respecting the different belief systems of various people."[79] With respect to epistemology, we must not subsume but *submit* to the Other insofar as we must be willing to put our beliefs to critical tests. We must remember that our theological formulations are always provisional; none of them catches the sacred fish.

Saving the Distinctives

The Angler admits that there are other sports, but he nevertheless is convinced that his sport (or art, or religion) is superior — "true" not just for him but for everyone. His task is to convince others, not through violent rhetoric or manipulation, but through persuasion, that the world as seen from his "angle" is possible, desirable, and true. A form of dialogue modeled

78. DiNoia, p. 169.
79. Kathryn Tanner, "Respect for Other Religions: A Christian Antidote to Colonialist Discourse," *Modern Theology* 9 (1993): 15.

on trinitarian life will be less concerned with the defense of a received inheritance (the doctrinal equivalent of the Persistence of the Past) than with exploring ways to "down the otherness" (the etymological meaning of *katallage* or "reconciliation") in a noncoercive manner. Such reconciliation can be bought only with a price, namely, our exposure to otherness, negativity — perhaps intellectual crucifixion. True dialogue demands the practice, and not simply the discourse, of Christian love. Indeed, might we not venture, in light of our trinitarian reflections, to suggest that it is *only* by opening ourselves up to the Other and to difference that we are true to our Christian distinctives?

The Incomplete Angler: Remaining Questions

I have been angling in the Rubicon, not crossing but standing, knee-deep, in its waters, trying to gain a perspective, casting questions. The following queries, about other positions as well as my own, continue to bait (and bite).

Love and the Other

What are the nature and scope of God's love for the Other? Does "God is love" entail a universal salvific will? Is there really nothing that will be excluded from the divine life? Will even the demonic be domesticated in a noncoercive way (and what biblical support is there for such a position)? And by what means are we caught up into the divine love: is it by virtue of God's being creator, or Savior, or simply Spirit?

Spirit and Son

Inclusivists and pluralists alike claim that the Spirit is universally active, and that therefore Christians must try to discern the Spirit in other religions. But if the Spirit's activity is really universal, then why restrict it to the world religions? And if the salvific will of God is truly universal, then we can no longer limit the means of salvation to the religions. How, then, can we discern God's Spirit, if it is indeed everywhere? Does not the narrative identification of the triune God present the Spirit as the Spirit of Christ — not simply the Logos, but the crucified and raised Christ? How else are we to take seriously verses such as John 8:39 ("for as yet the Spirit had not been given, because Jesus was not yet glorified"), not to mention the event of Pentecost itself? Is Hegel's universal *Geist* really *der Heilige Geist*? Perhaps it is time to reclaim the Reformed emphasis on the inseparability of Word and Spirit, and in particular its doctrine of the testimony of the Spirit, for a theology of religions?

The Identity of God, Again

Pluralism, insofar as it claims that the various names and predications for God are only modes of speaking about the same God, is guilty of semantic Sabellianism. Pannenberg, however, sees a continuing validity in the philosophical concept and generic term "God" as a minimal identifying description (e.g., God is the Being behind beings, the origin of the cosmos). To what extent, then, are the various religions about the "same" God?

We may agree with Pannenberg that the other religions, insofar as they recognize the one God (the Creator), have a true but not exhaustive identity description of God. It is partially true, and thus it has a relative adequacy — but how relative? how adequate? Carl Braaten expresses my concern: "One of the open questions for me at this time is how Pannenberg relates the christologically motivated Christian doctrine of the Trinity to the understanding of God in the other religions of the world."[80] Does the Muslim pray to the same God as the Christian? Pannenberg does not shirk the question, but he does not answer it either: "This is a question to be decided by God, not us."[81]

Conclusion

In conclusion: the Trinity is the Christian answer to the identity of God. The one creator God is Father, Son, and Spirit. This is an identification that is at once exclusivistic and pluralistic. And because this God who is three-

---

80. Braaten, "The Problem of the Absoluteness of Christianity," in *Worldview and Warrants*, p. 65. Or as he states it elsewhere: "The question is how the experience of God apart from Christ is related to the experience of God in Christ" ("The Place of Christianity among the World Religions: Pannenberg's Theology of Religions," in *The Theology of Wolfhart Pannenberg*, p. 310).

81. Pannenberg, "Religious Pluralism and Conflicting Truth Claims: The Problem of a Theology of the World Religions," in D'Costa, ed., *Christian Uniqueness Reconsidered*, p. 103.

in-one has covenanted with what is other than himself — the creature — the identity of God is also inclusivistic. The Trinity, far from being a *skandalon*, is rather the transcendental condition for interreligious dialogue, the ontological condition that permits us to take the other in all seriousness, without fear, and without violence.

In the course of Walton's work, the Angler convinces his dialogue partners, Hunter and Falconer, that angling is indeed the best recreation. He does not coerce, but persuades.[82] Rhetoric is part of the story: the Angler is both passionate and eloquent. But what he really does is *witness*, in his discourse and in his practice, to the nature of angling in such a way that its reality is disclosed to his listeners. He invites them to enter the angler's world, and they experience therein the freedom that comes from contemplation and from living in harmony with nature.

As the Apostle Paul notes, however, rivers are dangerous (1 Cor. 11:26). The Angler must be careful not to become engulfed in deep waters. But a river of life, identified in John 7:38-39 with the Spirit, runs through the city of God (Rev. 22:1). If this Spirit is universally available, it is not because all religions drink from the same great river. It is rather because the Spirit has sprung, under the conditions of history, from a Rock (1 Cor. 10:4). Life in the Spirit, "rivers of living water," shall flow from the hearts of those who believe in Jesus.

82. Cf. Paul Eddy's comment: "the question of tolerance or intolerance is one of *attitude*, not truth-claim" ("Paul Knitter's Theology of Religions: A Survey and Evangelical Response," *Evangelical Quarterly* 65 [1993]: 239).

• 5 •

Is There a Trinitarian Experience in Sufism?

ROLAND POUPIN

Introduction: A Warning

Since this subject engages us in interreligious dialogue, the approach I will develop could lead us to wonder whether this approach to Islam corresponds indeed to the real Islam, the Islam we know through Muslims we encounter? (I must clarify that my knowledge on this subject is not that of a specialist or a land missionary, but is only due to my reading of translations, orientalists, and islamacists). That is why it is necessary to remind ourselves of some central points, as a warning.

Contemporary dialogue between Christianity and other religions, particularly the Islamic-Christian dialogue, has a brief history. It began with the breaking down of many boundaries subsequent to the development of our modern world.

Classic Christianity — here, I am thinking more precisely of Roman Catholic Christendom and of Byzantine Christendom — presented itself as a political and religious entity, relatively insulated, which corresponded roughly to the ancient Roman Empire. It tolerated only Judaism as different (I am not speaking of heretics), and that in ghettos, waiting for expulsions.

Other churches, on the borders of the Middle Ages, were in different positions, sometimes conflicting positions, toward a growing Islam, which sometimes had the status of "millah," that is, "protected communities," a kind of ghetto.

There were yet other situations in between: think of Spain. In these intermediary situations, some dialogue happened to take place. For example, there was the Catalan Raymond Lull.

72

However, the ancient world did not experience the breakdown of walls that we know today. Concerning Western Christianity, the one from which we've come, a dialogue with other religions, and specifically with Islam, generally took the form of simple proselytizing or conflict.

This tendency still exists, and could be symbolized summarily by a confusion between Christ and the Church: "no one comes to the Father but through me" becoming "no one comes to the Father but through the Church," the Church perceived as the exclusive owner of grace. Proselytizing here becomes a duty, a virtual moral imperative, and then sometimes a dialogue of the deaf, that eventually evolves into dangerous ideological conflicts.

But the growing complexity of the modern world, following the fall of dividing walls become porous, has made such a vision too simplistic in the eyes of many Christians. Some adopt an attitude that may seem just as simplistic, which we could sum up as "tout va pour le mieux dans le meilleurs des mondes" ("everything is for the best in the best of all possible worlds") since "all roads lead to Rome."

Such a simplification doesn't satisfy everyone, not even Rome. Some synthesis of these two extremes can be found there: it is possible to find in all religion and culture potential sons of the Church.

Such an approach, *mutatis mutandis,* that is to say without the centrality of the ecclesial organism, can be found sometimes in Protestantism. But at the heart of Protestantism is another approach, stemming from Kierkegaard, and a Barthianism, derived from Luther — we could say it is inspired by 1 Corinthians 1 and 2, and by the general Pauline stance toward the Church of Jerusalem of that time. We will consider particularly this approach.

Christ, in his crucifixion, is the contradiction of all our attitudes of piety, even Christian ones. Yet God breaks in at the heart of our failures, religious failures among them. In a similar manner, God is near in many cultures, including Islam.

Such an approach, prompted by a desire to mediate, tries to consider the face of the neighbor, in this case a Muslim, the way in which we believe Christ would consider it. I will call this an "intercessory" approach. But let us not be mistaken by the fact that a Muslim as he is in himself, as we know him daily, could have some difficulties recognizing himself — claiming instead an image of himself that is often hard for us to understand.

However, keeping in mind that God is near Islam, among other cultures, will prevent us from caricatures, which we make too easily in the name of cold objectivity. While stressing what we think are points of meeting, we must bear in mind that the Islam we will consider here is rare.

Christian Discovery of Sufism

It is thus more precisely in Sufism that Islam may — according to this intercessory approach — astonish the theologian of the cross, of the transfiguration of failure.

This way of creating a dialogue through mediation would be an opportunity of discovering in the other the face of the crucified Christ. The "Pauline" approach that we spoke of is naturally not exclusive to Protestants. It was Louis Massignon, a Catholic thinker, who can be considered as a privileged witness — even initiator — of such an intercessory approach toward Islam. Louis Massignon introduced the Sufi al Hallâj (857-922 c.e.)[1] to the Western world and its Christianity.

Hallâj, in his quest for God, sought to actualize what he himself saw as being the blasphemy *par excellence*, the assimilation of the creature to God. This assimilation, paradoxical duty of the mystic, ends and fulfills itself in its punishment, martyrdom.

Hallâj was the originator of an important tradition of imitators of Jesus. This imitation consisted of a damnation, experienced as the encounter of God by his mystical lover, a scandalous encounter but one that becomes the full accomplishment of the supreme duty of the Muslim: the *Tawhîd*, or "unification of God," that is, the practice of the proclamation of divine unicity: "There is no God but God."

In one of his poems, Hallâj proclaims to God:

I want you, I want you not for the reward,
But I want you for the punishment
Because I obtained all that I desired
Except the delights of my passion in suffering.[2]

The desire expressed by Hallâj in this poem seems to be constant for him. It is the desire of martyrdom, the desire of the passion, in imitation of Jesus' passion, as it is expressed in a text written in the name of the famous Sufi (but attributed by critics to one of his disciples):

1. In his work *La passion d'al Hallâj* (Paris, 1922; repr. Gallimard, 1975).
2. Hallâj, *Poèmes mystiques,* trans. Sami-Ali (Paris: Sindbad, 1985), no. 6, p. 31.

As Jesus, I have arrived at the gibbet, taking care in all . . .
As Jesus, I have thrown myself down upon the Psalter,
I lifted the veil from the face of the ideas.
As Jesus, I rise from the dead.[3]

The Question of the Crucifixion

There is another question about the Muslim reading of the foundational facts of Christianity, which lies behind the Sufi's understanding of martyrdom, that we have to consider: the crucifixion of Christ.

We know that current theology of Islam rejects the idea of the historical crucifixion of Jesus. One could insist on this point, emphasizing that the idea of such a death of such a prophet is impossible for Islam to conceive.[4] This may allow us to stress the subject of the scandal that Hallâj was, even to the point of being put to death by members of his own religion, for there is no doubt that Hallâj believed in the crucifixion of Jesus, and he wanted to imitate him, particularly in his martyrdom. The cross, the place *par excellence* of the hallâjian imitation of Jesus!

The paradox is even deeper in Islam than in Christianity, as is made obvious by the common rejection of the idea of the historical crucifixion of Jesus and even more by the idea of the theoretical impossibility of such a crucifixion.

In this ultraparadoxical abyss the experience of Hallâj takes place. In it, he intends to unite himself to God. And we must not forget that the "assimilation" of a man to God is radically blasphemous in Islam, even as a simple epiphanic sign. But Hallâj seems to lead us toward such areas, to the total admiration of Louis Massignon.

The assimilation of the creature to God, which Hallâj seems to come close to, is even seen, according to one reading of a koranic text (XXVIII, 83), as the fault of the devil. From there a double imitation (of Jesus and of the devil) was often attributed to the famous Sufi.[5] But for him, there

---

3. In Michel Hayek, *Le Christ de l'islam* (Paris: Seuil, 1959), p. 233, a presentation and translation, in French, of Muslim texts on Christ.

4. Cf. G. C. Moucarry, "La crucifixion impossible," *Nuance,* Journal réformé évangélique, no. 26 (June–July 1992).

5. Accusation contested by Massignon, "Perspective transhistorique sur la vie de Hallâj," in *Parole donnée,* coll. 10/18 (Paris: René Julliard/U.G.E., 1962), p. 62sq. Published in introduction of the translation by Massignon of the al Hallâj *Dîwân,* coll. Points/Sagesses no. 44 [1955] (Paris: Seuil, 1981).

is no true proclamation of the unicity of God but in this blasphemy and its punishment, in this punishment-blasphemy.

Without it, the unification, the proclamation of the divine unicity, is only the abstract discourse of a creature who, while doing its abstract proclamation, is putting itself unconsciously as the other aspect of a duality persisting in front of God — while it is trying to define as one this undefinable one. The final purpose is to join in the act of God by which he unifies himself in his creatures; otherwise it would be only a definitive failure of the unification. So there is for the mystic no true *Tawhîd*, no true unification of God, but in a God who is Love-Lover-Beloved, loving himself in the eyes of the loving creature for the object of his love — and all the stronger the moment this love is exalted in death — a kind of definitive abolition of the duality between God and the creature. We will treat below the link of this love with "human" love. The death of Hallâj is claimed to be an imitation of Jesus' death.

Being thus inserted in a line acknowledging the cross of Jesus, Hallâj is in a tradition that is far from being an exception in primitive Islam, which, if we believe its own texts, granted rather readily the reality of the historical crucifixion of Jesus — hence interpreting the famous verse 157 of the fourth surat as a paradoxical glorification of Jesus on the cross — which seems very close to the Gospel of John, which here confirms a place par excellence for what we could call trinitarian revelation.

A Tradition in Islam Speaking of Jesus Crucified[6]

Indeed, the most common exegesis in our days of the koranic verse *shubbiha lahum* (Koran IV, 157) — "it *seemed* to them" (who wanted to kill him) that they had crucified him, but they were victims of an illusion — is that Jesus was not crucified. But this text was not always understood as signifying that he was not crucified. It is even probable, as we will briefly see, that primitive Islam generally made of this text another exegesis, and this in its main streams.

Two texts in the *Encyclopedia (Rasâ'il)* of the *Ikhwân al-Safa* make this line of interpretation explicit.

The first one (c. 934 c.e.), from Abu Hâtim Razi, affirms being founded on the teaching of a master — the reading is then older. Abu Hâtim says that the beginning of the verse

6. For this section, cf. my article "Exégèses anciennes de la sourate IV, 157-158, et christologie coranique," in *Etudes théologiques et religieuses* (1993).

does not deny at all the crucifixion and that it has to be interpreted while keeping in mind its ending: 'and they didn't kill truly *(yaqîna)*, God elevated him', and since Jesus died as a martyr, remembering the verses (II, 149; cf. III, 163) on the death of the martyrs: 'do not think of those who were killed in the way of God that they are dead: but that they are alive; in spite of the fact that you do not realise it'.[7]

The second text summarizes the doctrine of the *Ikhwân al-Safâ* concerning the death of Christ:

> his humanity was crucified and his two hands were nailed on the two woods of the cross. . . . Then he was buried. . . .
>
> Three days later, they met together in the place where he promised to appear to them. So they verified the authenticity of the signs covenanted between them.
>
> The news spread among the sons of Israel that Christ had not been killed. His tomb was opened, but his humanity was not there anymore. So the different sects argued over him. . . .[8]

The exegesis of the *falâsifa* ("philosophers") connects with the Ismailians'. So testifies Fakhr al Dîn Râzî (1209 c.e.) in his *tafsîr* (commentary on the Koran):

> The Nestorians think that Jesus was crucified in his humanity and not in his divinity. The majority of the philosophers opt for a similar point of view. . . . The soul of Jesus was particularly holy and celestial, flowing from divine lights, eminently close to angelic lights. Such a soul remains impassible before murder and destruction of the flesh. Separated from the flesh, it is liberated and rejoins the immensity of the Heaven.[9]

Hallâj is part of the same tradition. Two centuries later, Abu Hamid Ghazâli (1111 c.e.) still reads this verse in the same way. Ghazâli is a very significant personality in Sunnism. He is, according to the specialist Caspar, one of the three most influential personalities in Sunnism.[10]

---

7. Louis Massignon, "Le Christ dans les Evangiles selon Al-Ghazâli," *Opera minora*, t. II, Dar Al-Maaref (Liban), 1963 [*Revue des études islamiques*, 1932, cahier IV], p. 535 (appendice II : La mort du Christ en croix).

8. Hayek, p. 232.

9. Hayek, p. 230.

10. Robert Caspar, *Traité de théologie musulmane* (Rome, 1987), p. 219. The two others are Ibn 'Arabi (cf. *infra*) and Ibn Taymiyya (with whom we should go down till the fourteenth

Ghazâli admits material crucifixion. However, this exegesis does not appear unanimous in Islam; as Massignon noticed, Ghazâli is discreet on this point, adding when he speaks of it: "so say the Christians."[11]

In the thirteenth century C.E., such an exegesis seems to be the exegesis of Ibn 'Arabi (1240), who, along with Ghazâli, is one of the three most significant personalities in Sunnism, still according to Caspar — and we can add, the best representative of Islam's mystics.

The exegesis of Ibn 'Arabi is particularly enlightening. We can read in him two types of texts:

> When he (Muhammad, at the time of his ascension at night) came in (the second heaven), he saw Jesus in his body himself; because he didn't die until now, but Allah elevated him to heaven where he made for him a place to stay and where he placed him as judge.[12]

If this text could make one think of a noncrucifixion of Jesus, Ibn 'Arabi himself brings us to the necessity of understanding it another way. Commenting on the koranic verse in which we see Jesus saying "safety on me on the way of my birth, on the day of my death, and on the day of my resurrection" (XIX, 34), Ibn 'Arabi writes that this verse is to be related to the one on the crucifixion of Jesus (IV, 157), and he continues:

> So Jesus said to them safety was upon him on the day he died, safe from being slain. For if he had been slain, he would have been slain in martyrdom, and the martyr is alive, not dead, just as we have been prohibited from saying that, a command that still remains [in effect]. So Jesus gave news that he died and was not slain, since he mentioned safety upon him on the day he died.[13]

This leads us close to the Johannine consideration of the cross as a lifting up: "For Me, when I am lifted up from earth . . ." (John 12:32-33).

---

century, the time when the docetist reading of our koranic verse became quasi-unanimous), whom we will not consider.

11. Massignon, p. 534.

12. Hayek, p. 227.

13. Ibn 'Arabi, *Futûhat Makkiyya*, ch. 195, 388, 5, English translation by William C. Chittick, in *Les illuminations de La Mecque*, texts translated in French and in English (Paris: Sindbad, 1988), pp. 269-70.

The Damnation by Love

Around Hallâj, a whole tradition was developed, dedicating a great venera-
tion to this martyr of the love of God. Many Sufis and many Kurds, the
Yezidis, venerate Hallâj, and some of them, particularly the Yezidis, venerate
Iblis, the devil in the Koran, as well.[14]

This veneration of Hallâj and Iblis finds its historical beginning
among the apologists of the martyred Sufi, accused of having damned
himself as Iblis had.

According to the Koran, Iblis, cursed by God, shouted: "I testify to
your glory" (XXXVIII, 83). It was the great mystic Ahmad Ghazâli (1126),
the brother of Abu Hamid Ghazâli, who derived from this text the theme
of the devil damned by love.[15]

Ahmad Ghazâli belongs, through the Koran, to a tradition that goes
back to Origen's conception of an angelic fall, that of Lucifer, after an
allegorical reading of Ezekiel 28. This locates the origin of evil back to a
prehistorical sin committed by the most beautiful of angels.

Ahmad Ghazâli, in a very profound contemplative insight, finds in
this sin the love of the devil for the beauty of God, and the devil's wish to
be united to him who caused his curse (and according to the Yezidis, his
forgiveness).

The curse of Iblis according to this perspective is founded on a cause
similar to that of Hallâj's martyrdom. It is the suffering and the passion of
the impossible love. It is this impossibility that is sealed in the *fatwâ*, the
sentence of condemnation of Hallâj, in 922, which eventually would result
in his death.

The theology of Ibn Dawûd Ispahani (909),[16] a great jurist and mystic,
who sent a first *fatwâ* against Hallâj some years before, reveals the sin his
contemporaries accused him of having committed: the *tashbîh*, the assimilation of God to man, a sin against the *Tawhîd*, the proclamation of the
unicity of God. It is the desire of Hallâj itself that is condemned, the desire
of the union with God that is sealed in his passion.

Here Ibn Dawûd is probably very close to Hallâj. Ibn Dawûd recom-

---

14. Cf. Louis Massignon, "Les Yezidis du Mont Sindjar 'adorateurs d' Iblis,' " in *Satan*,
Etudes carmélitaines, coll. L'ordinaire (Desclée de Brouwer, 1948), pp. 133-34.
15. Cf. Henri Corbin, *Histoire de la philosophie islamique* (Paris: Gallimard, [1964–
1974] 1986), pp. 279 ss.
16. Cf. Corbin, *Histoire de la philosophie islamique*.

mended a nonconsummating love, for the purpose of perpetuating love's desire.

It is the ultimate exaltation of love such as the tribe of the Banû 'Odhra — the "virginalists" — experienced, according to the legend. Ibn Dawûd himself sang of this tribe, a tribe where "one died when he loved,"[17] in the way of the *hadîth:*

> He who loves, keeps his secret, stays chaste, and dies of love; he dies as a martyr.

Love of God and Human Love

The issue is that of a proximity, and a very close one, between this mystical love and "human" love. For the love of Iblis for God, according to the myth developed by Ahmad Ghazâli, and the same impossible love of God that the mystics endure, is very close to the suffering of the unaccomplished love of the lover for the beloved.

The whole problem is precisely the one of the relationship between human love and the love given to God. If the most careful of the Sufis see here a simple relation of transposition in a Platonic style, those who thirst most for God will see in this transposition itself the sign of a failure of the quest.

Indeed, for them, if there is only a strict typological transposition from the love of the creature to the love of God, duality subsists, the unification of God is unaccomplished in the creation.

For if the assimilation — the *tashbîh* (with its risks of pantheism, and even idolatrous tendencies) — is avoided, it is but for a purely *abstract* profession of the divine unicity — the *ta'tîl*. And this is what Hallâj or Ahmad Ghazâli refused. With them we may also mention Rûzbehân Baqlî Shirazi (1209), who develops more precisely the thought that sees the unveiling of God to Himself — the gaze of God upon Himself — in the gaze of the human lover on his beloved.[18]

It is also in this tradition that we find Ibn 'Arabi (1165–1240), who teaches with Rûzbehân that it is God

---

17. Corbin, *Histoire de la philosophie islamique.*
18. Cf. his *Jasmin des fidèles d'amour (Kitâb-e 'Abhar al-'ashiqîn),* tr. in French from Persian Henry Corbin, coll. "Islam Spirituel" (Paris: Verdier, 1991).

who manifests himself to each beloved and to the eyes of each lover. There is thus only one lover in universal existence (and it is God) so that the entire world is lover and beloved.[19]

As Rûzbehân, Ibn 'Arabi finds this teaching in this *hadîth:*

I was a (hidden) treasure; I wasn't known and I loved to be known. Thus I created the creature and I revealed myself to them in such a way that they knew me.[20]

And it is in the teaching of Ibn 'Arabi that we find the culmination of the understanding of Ahmad Ghazâli and of Rûzbehân of a tri-unity "love-lover-beloved" where "the lover and the beloved transsubstantiate themselves in the unity of the pure substance of love" to realize "the secret of the *Tawhîd*," that is the secret of unification.[21]

The gaze of the human lover upon his beloved, revealing itself as being the one of God upon himself, thus becomes the triune place of the unification of God, without which the unification, then purely abstract, appears illusory, the consecration of an unbreachable duality. It is ultimately up to the mystic to enter into this divine tri-unity, which is revealed in the human love, by becoming himself as it were the eye of God contemplating himself in the moment when the contemplated and the contemplator become one and the same — just as the butterfly becomes one with the flame to which he is united when the flame consumes the duality that separated them, to take an image from Ahmad Ghazâli.

What his followers say in such an astonishing way concerning the revealing relationship of the human lover and the human beloved, for an unveiling of God that culminates in martyrdom, Hallâj experienced in his own flesh, with the drama and the curse for an immediate love of God, in a way that is not without common points with that of the Iblis of Ahmad Ghazâli. Here, what the beauty of the human creature contemplated through the eyes of his lover reveals to God his own beauty, Hallâj unveils in the culminating moment of his punishment, his martyrdom and his damnation:

Like the butterfly which became the lover of the flame, . . . it has to

---

19. Ibn 'Arabi, *Traité de l'amour,* tr. M. Gloton, coll. "Spiritualités vivantes" (Paris: Albin Michel, 1986), p. 59.

20. Ibn 'Arabi, p. 59.

21. Corbin, p. 281.

continue to fly until it joins the flame. For a brief instant, it becomes itself its own beloved (since it [the butterfly] is the flame). And this is its perfection.[22]

Hallâj obtains at the heart of his curse, of his punishment, the "desired delights of his passion in suffering." He dies, in the sought after manner of Jesus, "having become a curse, according to which is written: cursed is the one who is hanged to the wood" (Gal. 3:13; Deut. 21:23); abandoned by God himself (Mark 15:34).

In this, and more precisely in his martyrdom, the mystic proves to be the subject of an encounter of God with himself, the lover thus becoming the mirror of a God finally unified by his creature; being then proclaimed the one and the only one by his martyr lover, annihilated in his martyrdom: God alone subsists as being himself love, lover, and beloved.

Henry Corbin, another great spokesman, with Massignon, of Islamic mysticism in the West, is the one who brilliantly highlighted this theme of Sufism.

*   *   *

Concerning the psychological dimension of which we must speak, we could ask if such an exaltation of the impossible does not simply proceed from a neurosis.

A Freudian would probably point out all the elements of the castration complex, underlining the revindication of the *odhrit* love, necessarily unaccomplished, root of tensions clearly unbearable since they lead to death.

The psychological question eventually becomes more evident by the reading of the work of Denis de Rougemont. In his book *L'amour et l'Occident*,[23] Rougemont, analyzing the myth of Tristan and Isolde, states that the mutual love of Tristan for Isolde is nothing else than a narcissistic search for oneself through the other and not love of the other, desire of an encounter. And naturally, when speaking of a search for the unification of God, and of a participation in this unification of God, the question of narcissism, of a will to totality, is clearly put.

In the work of Rougemont, this neurotic narcissism issues forth in

---

22. Ahmad Ghazâli, *Les intuitions des fidèles d'amour*, ch. 39, cited in Corbin, p. 282.
23. *L'amour et l'Occident*, coll. 10/18 (Paris: Plon/U.G.E., 1972).

the encounter of oneself in death, ultimately only sought through the inaccessible other. And death in pursuing the inaccessible reality is indeed what befell Hallâj. So, is there here nothing but sick, masochist, narcissism? The risk does exist.

The alternative to such a diagnostic of neurotic narcissism is, on the contrary, to find a transgression of the narcissism that is tempting us all necessarily in our quest for the divine — and through this transgression a paradoxical victory over this unavoidable narcissism.

This unavoidable narcissism appears in all its reality in the legend of the "hallâjian" devil that we are all imitating. Being in totality with God, becoming one with the preexistential root of our being, is such a temptation that we sometimes confusedly see in it a kind of paradisaic hope — cf. Job 3, Jeremiah 20, Baudelaire in "Bénédiction," or Cioran, writing about "l'inconvénient d'être né," the inconvenience of being born. As it happens, instead of pursuing this hope, Hallâj is perhaps assuming it before passing over it, before recognizing it as being definitely impossible, joining in another way the Bible prophets passing through their trials (Job, Jeremiah). Here we see in what way his steps do not lead simply toward an assimilation to God.

The impossibility of fusion is the certainty of the failure of which Hallâj dies. Not because he might find himself again in God through death, but because of a definitive loss of the illusion of the totality. So the persistent maintenance of the nonencounter of the other — and notably of the venerated woman, given that mystics themselves generally married (Hallâj was father of four children) — this nonencounter may also be seen as a concrete recognition of the fact that there is an irreducible alterity, a definitive nontotality of our beings, which, far from being resolved in death, here becomes on the contrary clearly unavoidable. Here again appears the proximity of Hallâj and Ibn Dawûd who obtained his condemnation.

The martyrdom of Hallâj, an imitation of Jesus', and a symbol of the essential experience of the Sufis, would prove to be a definitive proclamation of an irreducible alterity, even in God himself, which is clearly trinitarian: definitive alterity, in eternity, of the unique God — Love, Lover, Beloved — tri-unity in which the disciple is called to enter to realize the *Tawhîd*, the proclamation of the unity of God. We can't avoid noticing a certain closeness to the Gospel of John: "we will come to him and make our home with him" (John 14:23); "that they may be one even as we are one — I in them and thou in me" (John 17:22-23).

The Respective Specificity of the Two Perspectives

Having said this, one should not neglect a remaining difference between *this* experience and the Christian one of the trinitarian life.

This difference could be illustrated with reference to what became of the inheritance of courtly love in the West, according to Rougemont in his book *L'amour et l'Occident*. Denis de Rougemont shows how the West went from a courtly ideal to romantic love because of a secularization of perspectives and of a loss of sight of the mystical dimension of medieval love. The beloved doesn't anymore reveal to the lover his divine foundation, his ideal to which he corresponds.

We can't avoid noticing as well, in parallel, that Western philosophy came to profess that the Idea does not exist in itself, that it is a name, an instrument of the thinking subject. Hence is is not by chance that love is seen in modern times as a subjective phenomenon, the beauty of the beloved having its ground not in the divine Idea, but in the individual psychology of the lover. Likewise the phenomenon of love's "crystallization" according to Stendhal: a purely subjective phenomenon, the lover, in a way, *producing* the beauty of the object of his love.

After this, platonic love becomes nothing but a neurotic sublimation of a biological desire.

Such a derivation of perspective proper to the West may find its origin in the exaltation toward an ineffable transcendence of the ideal relationship of love, lover, and beloved — a transcendence that occasions a skepticism that Sufism did not know.

For the difference between the two perspectives, Christian and Sufi, could be linked precisely to the fact that, as we know, Christianity stands for a distinction between the inner trinitarian life of God (the immanent or the ontological Trinity) and Trinity in relationship to the world (the economical Trinity).

Hence, where Islamic dogma only recognizes the transcendence of the One, Christianity stands also for keeping the triune life of the One in the same transcendence; hence the trinitarian life of the One is itself apophatic. Consequently, the divine ideas manifested in the creation are also implicated in negative theology, whereas Sufism considers ideas as the immanent presence of the transcendent God to the world — which is why it was attacked by the rest of Islam. However, we must not see in this immanence a pantheism: to this end Henry Corbin insists on the necessity of not losing sight of the distinction between "Being" *(l'Etre)* and "existents" *(les étants):* "there is in Being *(l'Etre)* (in the act-to be) only God. Which does not at all mean that there is, as existent *(étant)*, only God."[24]

The point of contact between the ontological transcendental Trinity of Christianity and the experiential tri-unity of the *Tawhîd* of Sufism might be indirectly suggested by Henry Corbin. Corbin compares Avicenna's angelology in its aspect of the emanation of the ten celestial Intelligences to the cabalistic teaching on the ten *Sephirôth*. Henry Corbin observes that the "eclosion of the *Sephirôth* accomplishes itself ontologically and theosophically before the one of the hierarchy of the Intelligences. The *Sephirôth* would be in a certain way the temple where the ten Intelligences have their respective place."[25] *Mutatis mutandis,* we could suggest that the ontological Trinity is the Temple of the tri-unitarian experience.

The experiential tri-unity of Sufism comes so close to the Christian doctrine of the Trinity in its economical aspect that one may wonder where were the points of contact or influences. Henry Corbin willingly sees such points of contact through the ternary rhythms of Proclus's Neoplatonic angelology — which influenced Christianity as well as Islam.[26]

Asin Palacios, the Spanish specialist of Islam, in a famous study of Ibn 'Arabi writes that Sufism is an heir of Christian monasticism, an influence culminating in the work of Ibn 'Arabi, who — let's not forget — sees, not in Mohammad, "simple" seal of the prophets, but rather in Jesus the seal of "holiness," of "friendship with God." For Palacios, Hallâj's experience is that of the Pauline formula: "it is Christ who lives in me."[27] In Islam, a path could have developed through which "the negation of those two dogmas, the trinitarian and the theandric, would have been slowly erased by the work of sufi theologians, culminating in this attitude of Ibn 'Arabi."[28]

In order to avoid having to decide between possible influences, perhaps we should be content to state that there does exist a thirst for God that leads to a tri-unitarian experience.

So, in Sufism, the perceptible beauty of human creatures is in itself a manifestation of God and places us immediately on a level of being that Henry Corbin calls "imaginal." For it is not the beautiful human being who

24. Henri Corbin, *Le paradoxe du monothéisme,* coll. Biblio essais (Paris: L'Herne/Le livre de poche, 1981), pp. 14-15.

25. Corbin, *Le paradoxe du monothéisme,* p. 135.

26. Corbin, *Le paradoxe du monothéisme,* pp. 96sq., 100-102.

27. Miguel Asin Palacios, *L'islam christianisé, étude sur le soufisme d'Ibn 'Arabi de Murcie,* tr. in French from Spanish Bernard Dubant (Paris: Ed. de la Maisnie, 1982), p. 196.

28. Palacios, p. 204.

is epiphanic, but the *beauty* of this human being. It is not less the perceptible beauty itself that is epiphanic. A *hadith* sees the Prophet saying: "I saw my God in the most beautiful of forms," that is, human.

As for classical Christianity, the human being is conceived as being in the image of God; this form has an objective reality — we can speak of realism of universals.

Therefore, the perception of the perceptible beauty of a beautiful human creature is received not only as being due to the perception of the historical, terrestrial contemplator, but as being an objective reality, founded in God. It is perceived by the terrestrial subject, whose gaze unites with the gaze of God, from whom the beauty of the creature comes. This is the ground of the Sufis' platonic love. Prophets — and often Jesus, but of course in a less exclusive way than in Christianity — here become creatures of explicit beauty, in which God manifests his beauty — one thinks of the *hadith:* "God is beautiful and loves beauty."

If Christianity — while insisting on the full realization of this beauty in Jesus — could appropriate such a perspective, it would be by nuancing it: by the fact that the ideal beauty transcends the physical beauty to the point where the apparent absence of physical beauty is the paradoxical place of manifestation of divine beauty. This may be discovered by the contemplation of faith, which sees the beauty of God in the ugliness of the crucified, through an aesthetic parallel with First Corinthians, where the wisdom and power of God are seen in the apparent foolishness and weakness of the Cross. We should, however, not accentuate too much this difference, since, in a similar way, the tortured Hallâj is perceived as unveiling the beauty of God at the very moment his martyrdom disfigures him.

To Conclude: A Trinitarian Experience?

Let us remind ourselves that it is only with a possible *experience* of a trinitarian type that we are concerned, and no more.

In this we will keep to the distinction established by Christian theology between the economic Trinity and the ontological Trinity. Islam, let us not forget, refuses the idea of a trinity, and thus of an ontological Trinity — with its relative Christology — a fact on which Henry Corbin rightly insists.

Having emphasized this fact without any ambiguity, one can only wonder if the experience of failure, and the idea of transfigured failure, in Sufism is not a way of conceiving what could be a close experience of the economical aspect of the trinitarian life, manifested most precisely in the cross.

A theology of failure. A transfigurative paradox on which Paul founds the enlargement of the hebraic ritual of primitive Christianity: Christ is the contradiction of all the rituals of the Judeo-Christian ritual as much as of the pagan religious experiences.

Without giving a definitive answer to the question of a possible trinitarian experience in Sufism, we must nevertheless see here the place of a radical interrogation, made by the cross, to our own incessant recurrent pretensions to be masters, or even trustees, of a grace that comes to us only, and precisely, by *dis*possessing us.

6

The Trinity, Natural Theology, and a Theology of Nature

COLIN GUNTON

The Question in Context

"Pluralism" is a highly ambiguous, if not equivocal, term. It can denote the presence of competing worldviews and doctrines in a culture or era, or it can mean relativist pluralism, according to which the plurality of options entails that there can be no truth, only various perspectives upon the world, or that all doctrines and claims are perspectives on the one underlying reality, which is the same for all but differently expressed. In that sense, the modern situation is not a new one, being largely a republication of Protagoras's view that truth is relative to the perceiver. But it is new in the sense that modern dogmatic pluralism is the fruit of the particular intellectual and cultural developments that have made the modern condition what it characteristically is. It might even be said that modern relativist pluralism arises out of, as a reaction against, excessively unitary claims for the validity of certain accounts of the knowing process. I shall illustrate this claim later in the paper.

But first, to anticipate two major contentions of the paper as a whole. Theology has to do with foundations and with unity. Of the former it has to be said that it has to do with the fact, if it is a fact, that things are what they are because God has made and is making them to be so. Whatever we make of foundationalism, without a foundation, that is, without a doctrine

An earlier version of this essay was published in Colin Gunton, *A Brief Theology of Revelation* (Edinburgh: T & T Clark, 1995).

of creation, the rest of what we say is pointless. Therefore it cannot concede an inch to modern dogmatic pluralism without subverting its own basis. To flirt with postmodernism in some of its forms is to invite disaster. Of the latter — unity — it is the case that the doctrine of God serves, among other things, to give an account of why things hold together, why there is one world. Pluralism in its dottier manifestations cannot take account of the fact of the essential unity of our experience: of the fact that fire burns and water drowns, of the fact that the same laws of nature hold in all parts of the universe. The Christian account of the matter is that the foundations and the unity of things rest on Jesus Christ, the one Word of God through whom the Father created, upholds, and redeems all that is. Otherwise put, the doctrine of the Trinity is concerned with unity in plurality, not an absolute pluralism. In the remainder of this paper I hope to engage with this matter through the focus provided by the distinction between a natural theology and a theology of nature.

General Revelation

If there is a unity to human experience of the world, one way of understanding it is to say that the creation in some way reveals its single creator. To put it another way, we can say that the function of the doctrine of general revelation is to hold to the biblical teaching, clearly expressed in Romans 1:19-20, as well as in some of the Psalms, that God's eternal power and deity are made known in the things that have been made. The creator is revealed in and by the creation. But the status and function of such knowledge is the source of immense differences in the tradition. On the one hand, it is linked to the question of so-called natural theology, by which is meant the knowledge of God that is obtainable independently of revelation. But which revelation? Does not Romans 1 speak of a kind of revelation? But what is its relation to reason? That both Calvin and Barth can in different ways rightly call attention to the limits of unaided human knowledge of God, indeed to its negative value, by appealing to the context of the Pauline text — that it is preceded by a strong assertion of the wrath of God and succeeded by an analysis of first Gentile and then Jewish sin — shows the heart of the problem here. (In that respect, we might say that pluralism is a function of human fallenness, and the resulting incapacity to recognize things for what they are.)

On the other hand, and it can be said that this is the same problem in different guise, we meet here the specific problem of the relation of the doctrines of general revelation and creation. Barth has reminded us that the doctrine of creation is as much a doctrine of the creed, is as much the product of revelation, as the other doctrines of the faith. But that has not been the view of the mainstream medieval tradition against the background of which we still do so much of our theological thinking. For Aquinas, something like a doctrine of creation is developed before he approaches the specifically Christian teaching of creation out of nothing, which is in any case never of as much interest to him, and certainly not of as much interest to those who build upon him. If we are to understand the question of general revelation, we must therefore draw a distinction between a theology of nature and a natural theology. And the fact that the matter is by no means as simple as Barth may appear to have made it is indicated by the fact that, although he has a doctrine of creation, there is reason to suppose that he does not have much of a theology of nature, and this suggests that he, too, failed adequately to distinguish between natural theology and a theology of nature. We shall meet this problem later.

In the context of the modern debate about revelation and theology a third question is also now being insistently asked. It is that of foundationalism. What is foundationalism? Broadly speaking, it is the belief that there must be universal and common foundations for anything claiming to be thought, or authentically "scientific." The foundationalism that is so much in dispute today is that which belongs to what Alasdair MacIntyre, after Habermas, labeled the Enlightenment project.[1] It has taken two forms, the pure rationalist, which, in the formulation descending from Descartes, requires that all claims for truth base themselves on universally agreed conceptual foundations, and the empirical-rationalist, descending from Locke, which replaces the pure concepts of the Cartesian doctrine with the incorrigible data of experience. The best-known recent discussion of foundationalism in relation to the doctrine of revelation is that of Ronald Thiemann, who, in *Revelation and Theology,* accuses three representative modern theologians of foundationalism, meaning by it an attempt to base revelation on intuited foundations that are in some respect foreign — extrinsic — to that which they seek to base.[2]

His alternative, as is again too well known to require rehearsal, is to appeal to a form of narrative theology, in which God is co-given with the

1. Alasdair MacIntyre, *After Virtue* (Notre Dame: University of Notre Dame Press, 1981).
2. Ronald Thiemann, *Revelation and Theology: The Gospel as Narrated Promise* (Notre Dame: University of Notre Dame Press, 1987).

narrative in such a way that an external foundation is not required. There are a number of reasons why this approach is inadequate. One that is relevant to our concern with pluralism is that to base a theology in narrative is to preclude any discussion of the grounds for preferring one narrative to another, whether in question are rival versions of the Christian narrative — and they will, of course, be various, especially under modern conditions — or the narratives told by different religions. That may appear to be a recipe for tolerance. If all that I can claim is to have what seems to me to be a better narrative than, say, the Buddhists', am I not bound to live in peace with my partners in conversation? But the question makes a wrong assumption, and that is that relativism leads to peace. It does not, because not only does it evade the prior — logically prior — question of whether and in what sense what we say is true, but also increases the likelihood of violent conflict. If we in effect abandon any appeal to universal and common standards of humanity or rationality on the basis of which we may communicate and discuss our differences with our neighbor, a dialogue of the deaf is likely to eventuate.

The dispute about foundationalism is therefore more than a merely intellectual or "academic" dispute, for it brings into the center the question of the basis of our common human life on earth and the institutions that form the framework for that life. It is for that reason that the Enlightenment's commitment to universal and objective truth is much to be preferred to the fragmented world of postmodernism, in which there is no reason why we should bother to speak to each other expecting to be understood. What, then, is wrong with foundationalism? Not, it seems to me, that it seeks a common basis for rationality, but that it seeks the wrong one and in the wrong way. It seeks the wrong basis, because it seeks one that is merely secular:[3] something inherent within human reason and experience. It thus expects human reason to ground itself. It seeks it in the wrong way, because it believes that it can find what it wants apart from revelation. Another way of putting the matter would be to say that it is intellectually Pelagian, believing that it can found something eternally and universally true on human rational and scientific effort alone.

---

3. Whether Descartes's foundations in the innate ideas can rightly be described as secular is, of course, doubtful. But there is a secularizing direction, in that the source of revelation is to be found in himself, in the contents of his mind as it now is, i.e., as essentially unfallen and thus understood rather differently from the account in Romans 1. Their essential inadequacy was recognized by Kant, whose solution only served to exacerbate the problem. As the archmodern foundationalist, Kant attempted to found scientific culture in the timeless structures of the cognizing mind, an enterprise Hegel soon claimed to be viciously foundationalist and procrustean, only to found a more radical form of idealism himself.

But that only opens up a further question, merely alluded to in Thiemann's treatment. How far is a narratively identified God to be conceived as equivalent to a doctrine of God? We cannot in all this avoid the question of ontology, the question of who and what kind of being is the God supposedly made known narratively. If we are to approach an answer to the question, Why one narrative rather than another? we cannot be content with a deity merely economically identified, a God known merely in narrative, revelation, and the rest. The reason is this. The concept of God is intrinsically universal. It is not simply a question of juxtaposing various narratives in which God is allegedly identified, because of the inherently imperialistic connotations of the concept with which we are dealing. However else also we may wish to understand the idea of God, we cannot, I believe, evade the fundamental implications of the concept of God as the one who is the source of all being, meaning, and truth. Therefore, all claims for truth in some way or other have their basis in him. That is why I believe that the denial of the concept of objective truth — however that objectivity be understood — is tantamount to a denial of belief in God, as some postmodernists have realized. To invert Dostoyevsky's famous saying, if everything is permitted, then there is no God. The obverse is that the notion that God exists generates a concept of objective truth, and therefore believers must face up to the questions of the conflict of claims and the criteria for choosing one alleged truth rather than another. If my story differs from yours at a fundamental level, then at least one of us has got things wrong.

At one level, that is a matter of logic, that A and not-A cannot both be true: either Jesus is the savior of the world, or he is not; and if he is, then others cannot be. But the fact that some do not accept the claims of logic in this matter, and become for various reasons radical relativists, for example, shows that far deeper matters than logic, important though that is, are at stake. To approach the chief one, let me ask a number of questions that, though not merely rhetorical, are probably unanswerable, at least in a direct sense. Why did the Enlightenment quest for a merely secular theory of universal meaning and truth generate the doomed project now known as foundationalism? Why has the failure of that quest in turn convinced so many, against the apparent requirements of logic, that there is no truth, only a series of finally solipsistic expressions of opinion? I believe that the failure is essentially a theological one, and its center is to be found not so much in the doctrine of God as in the closely related doctrine of creation. Next I shall ask why things have come to the pass that they apparently have, and then return to the interlinked questions with which we are concerned: the questions of general revelation, of the doctrine of creation, and of the structures of universal rationality.

The God Made Known in Creation

As we have already seen, the question of general revelation is closely linked to the doctrine of creation. General revelation is the revelation of God through the things that have been made, through the creation. The roots of the modern problem are to be found in the history of the doctrine of creation and its fate in the medieval world. In summary, what happened was that reason came to be identified with a particular form of reason, and the doctrine of creation as the project of that particular form of reason, so that the doctrine of creation became associated with a particular form of philosophy. The defeat of a philosophical tradition, particularly by science, inevitably came to be seen as a defeat for the doctrine of creation.

We can approach our topic by asking, Why was the discussion of universals of such immense importance for medieval theology? It was not simply a matter of Plato against Aristotle, conceptual realism against nominalism, but underlying it were the two functions that the Platonic doctrine of forms and its Aristotelian equivalent performed in the medieval understanding of creation. First there was the ontological function. The forms, *rationes,* and so on performed a structuring, relational, framework for the created order: they were conceived as those things that held together the particulars of our experience. The founders of medieval ontology were therefore Philo and Augustine, who transferred the eternal Platonic forms from "external" reality to the mind of God. Effectively this crowded out the trinitarian, and particularly Christological, mediation of the doctrine of creation. The New Testament revelation is here unanimous: the structure — inscape — of creation is provided by the mediation of the Word through whom the world was made, according to John, the Son of the parallel conception of the Letter to the Hebrews and of the Pauline expressions of the cosmic work of Christ. The Philonic and Augustinian development means that the coeternal and personal mediator of God's creating work is effectively replaced by the *almost* eternal Platonic forms. The Logos is crowded out by the logoi.[4]

This is far from being a merely linguistic point. The notion of the

---

4. This is not to say there is no room for logoi as the rationality of created things. The problem comes when they are treated as in some way eternal or semidivine. "Ideas are principal forms or stable and unchangeable essences of things. They are themselves not formed, and they are eternal and always in the same state because they are contained in God's intelligence. They neither come into being nor do they pass away, but everything that can or does come into being and pass away is formed in accordance with them." Augustine, *De Div. Quaest.* 83, 46, 1-2.

Christological mediation of creation is, as Augustine realized in one of his rare appeals to trinitarian thought in this connection, crucial to an understanding of creation as both distinct from and related to its creator. The outcome of the effective redundancy of Christology for the doctrine of creation is thus, as a number of commentators have noted, a twofold contamination of the doctrine of creation. On the one hand, there emerged the scarcely consistent notion of eternally created reality, the forms in the mind of God, a notion going back to Origen, and this endangers the unity and transcendence of God. Harnack, as perceptive as ever, saw this clearly.[5] On the other hand, the understanding of the *whole* universe as created was thrown into doubt by the introduction within it of Neoplatonic notions of graded being. Some of the creation was truly finite and contingent, but other aspects, such as the heavenly bodies, still participated in a form of divinity and eternity. Thus the displacement of Christ by the forms or *rationes* brought about the contamination of the Christian doctrine of creation with pagan hierarchies of being, and therefore led to its effective obsolescence.

The second function performed by the Platonic-Aristotelian notions was, of course, rational and epistemological. An immediate, or near immediate, relation of the rational mind with divine rationality was posited, and its effect was to replace a doctrine of creation mediated by revelation with one directly or indirectly discovered by the human mind. The mediator of creation is not *Christus creator;* nor, as we shall see, is the mediator of *knowledge* of creation the creator Spirit. In both cases, the function is displaced to immanent realities: the continuity between reason and God mediated by semidivine forms. In this way the doctrine of creation was confused with natural theology, and became almost as a whole the function of general and not historical revelation. One effect of this was to entrench further the already well-established divorce of creation from redemption in Western theology, a connection vainly sought by Barth in his proposal to subordinate both creation and reconciliation to covenant and election.[6] (The awareness of that is one of the moments of truth in the so-called creation spirituality.) In the terms of the trinitarian interpretation being attempted here, we can therefore add to the Christological point of the previous paragraph the pneumatological one, that according to the scheme of the medieval synthesis, human

---

5. Adolph Harnack, *History of Dogma*, vol. 6, tr. W. McGilchrist (London: Williams and Norgate, 1899), pp. 184-85.

6. This does indeed connect the two, but at the price of subordinating creation to a higher-level version of salvation.

reason[7] effectively displaces the Holy Spirit as the mediator of the knowledge of creation.[8] In this respect, the apparent differences between Calvin and Barth on the subject of natural theology become irrelevant to the main point, which is that for a knowledge of God the creator, both the Bible as the source of revelation and the Holy Spirit as its mediator are required.[9]

A number of commentators have pointed out the implications of this displacement, particularly as it affected the development of modern science and culture.[10] The chief problem for theology was that the late medieval and early modern critique of the synthesis, in which it fell apart under the weight of its own tensions, was catastrophic for Christian theology, much of whose fate was to be rejected along with the Platonic-Aristotelian world-view with which it had been so closely tied. But there is more. The critique of medieval rationality that subverted the Christianity of which it had been the support in due time brought about also the modern crisis of rationality by seeking for culture a basis that was not that of the doctrine of creation.[11]

It will be instructive for our purpose to trace some episodes in the complex and many-sided developments that brought things to their present pass. The destruction of the synthesis can be seen especially, first, in the

7. Albeit human reason understood not as the Enlightenment took it, but as part of a unified Christian approach to truth. "The idea of *creation,* therefore, is the basic albeit unexplicated theological presupposition of both philosophical and revealed theology . . . ; and it underlines the ultimately theological (not philosophical) character of the whole enterprise." Ingolf U. Dalferth, *Theology and Philosophy* (Oxford: Blackwell, 1988), p. 74.

8. The chief weakness of those theories that concentrate attention on rational structures of a Platonic or Aristotelian kind is not only that they are limited in what they consider to be rational, but that they restrict that which may be considered revelatory. In contrast, a doctrine of creation that is trinitarianly articulated will, because it is Christological, have room for the rationality and revelatory quality of material things, and, because it is pneumatological, understand the potentiality for revelation of all aspects of the created world.

9. The differences between the two are best characterized by the fact that for Calvin, as he frequently laments, "not one in a hundred" realize the possibility of knowing God from his general revelation; for Barth, no one can. Whether this amounts to a practical difference is scarcely worth bothering about in comparison to the major pneumatological matter at stake.

10. See Hans Blumenberg, *The Legitimacy of the Modern Age,* tr. R. M. Wallace (Cambridge, MA, and London: MIT Press, 1983); Michael Buckley, *At the Origins of Modern Atheism* (New Haven and London: Yale University Press, 1987); and Harold Nebelsick, *The Renaissance, the Reformation and the Rise of Science* (Edinburgh: T & T Clark, 1992).

11. Here it is worth alluding to the brilliance of Hegel's insight that in the doctrine of the Trinity is to be found the clue to the unity of things. The problem is that by making human reason the locus of divine revelation, he simply reinvented the problem. Revelation is again replaced by reason, and it is no accident that there are echoes of both Neoplatonic emanationism and an Aristotelian self-thinking God in his recasting of Christianity.

95

displacement of the forms by Scotus from the mind of God and into the created world and, second, in the teaching of Ockham that the forms do not exist even for God. Ockham's effective abolition of metaphysics and its replacement by an appeal to authoritative revelation may appear to support my move from a doctrine of creation as natural theology to its placing in the system of revealed theology. But for a number of reasons this will not be the claim. First, because it subverted the rationality of theology, Ockham's revolution did the opposite of what I would seek. The doctrine of creation is, I believe, both the product of revelation and the basis for the universal rationality that both theology and modern culture must seek if disaster is not to strike. Any merely voluntarist and authoritative theology of revelation must be avoided if our concern is with that which we are taught by the Spirit of truth. Rather, as it turned out, the destruction of the Platonic-Aristotelian framework was also the destruction of the rationality of theology and ultimately that of all culture.

Second, the evidence suggests that Ockham's nominalistic theology served in the long term to subvert rather than to establish the doctrine of creation, by displacing the center of meaning and truth from the divine to the human creator. In that respect, Ockham is the source of, not the solution to, the worst of the problems of modernity. This is well illustrated by the thesis of Hans Blumenberg that modernity arises when the basis of rationality is displaced from divine to human agency. The arbitrary will of the Ockhamist deity is transferred to the arbitrary will of the human agent. Blumenberg welcomes the development, but it can be argued against him that it is the root of the current irrationalism and fragmentation that bears the name of postmodernism. If each individual human being is a separate source of rationality, then the collapse of all communication and community can only be around the corner. (At least it would be but for the residual common sense that will prevent people from swallowing the more absurd flights of postmodern dogma.)

It is in two features of the thought of Duns Scotus, in which, albeit sketchily, he returns to aspects of a revealed theology of creation, that the promise of more satisfactory developments are to be sought. The first is his doctrine of the univocity of the concept of being. What does this mean? Simply, that there are not degrees of being, but things just are. To say that God is and to say that the world is are not two different kinds of judgment, even though they concern distinctly the infinite and finite realms. There is good reason to believe that this is a peculiarly Christian teaching, at once the fruit of revelation and, as Harold Nebelsick has recently argued, one of the doctrines whose recovery made modern science possible. In what sense is it the fruit of revelation? It is a peculiarly Christian theological insight that there are not degrees of being, but a duality. There is God, and there is creation.[12] To repeat the modern example I have used already, modern science could not develop until the defeat of the doctrine that the heavenly bodies were of a different substance from the earthly. Aristotelianism taught that they were eternal, and therefore belonged on a hierarchy of being. Nebelsick points out that Philoponos as early as the sixth century had taught that

> the cosmos as a whole was composed of the *same kind of matter* and was subject to the same laws. Hence he both rejected the dichotomy between the *finite earthly* and the *infinite eternal* heavenly realms and recognised the importance of earthly reality. Further, Philoponos . . . insisted that nature could not be understood as the finite representation of infinite reality, but as real in itself.

Here we return to the problem of natural theology, indeed to its heart. If nature is to be understood no longer as the finite representation of infinite reality, but in *secular* terms, in its own right, in what sense can it be said to be revelatory of God? How shall we be able to say with Paul that God's eternal power and deity are revealed in the things that have been made? Some treatment of that question will be attempted below.

But, before that, let us consider the second of Scotus's contributions, and the one most tantalizing in its formulation, that is, his famous disagreement with Thomas Aquinas over Christology. As is well known, Scotus, in disagreement with Aquinas, taught that there would have been an incarnation even if Adam had not fallen. One of the reasons Aquinas gives for

---

12. Robert Jenson some time ago indicated the general character of the innovation in ontology that trinitarian thought made possible:

> The ontology of late antiquity had as its key operating principle the idea of degrees of being, the idea that there are sorts of entities distinguished from each other by being more or less real, by reflecting God's nature at fewer or more removes. . . . Gregory [of Nyssa] denies the whole principle. So far as "being" is concerned, a thing either is or is not, and that is all. . . .
>
> Eunomius shows how he can speak of degrees of being, when he calls "being" a "value-predicate." . . . Gregory is indignant at the notion that being is a value. "Whoever thought of such a thing?" he asks. Now of course the entire ancient world thought just such a thing. . . .
>
> Thus the whole ontological scheme is redone by Gregory. There are no degrees of being. There are simply different sorts of being, distinguished not by degree but simply by difference.

Robert Jenson, *God After God: The God of the Past and the God of the Future, Seen in the Work of Karl Barth* (Indianapolis and New York: Bobbs-Merrill, 1969), p. 120.

denying the speculation that the Incarnation would have happened even if there had been no sin is that creation is naturally ordered to God. Because he had Aristotle, Aquinas did not need a Christological mediation of the doctrine of creation. Scotus's opposing view that Christ is definitive for the relation of God to the whole world at least opens up the possibility of a return to a Christological mediation of creation, as both T. F. Torrance and Nebelsick have suggested. And this returns us to the claim with which I am concerned. The doctrine of creation is the fruit of revelation, biblical and Christological revelation, indeed. What the modern development achieves is the destruction of the logical link between the doctrine of creation and natural theology.[13] General revelation and natural theology are two quite distinct categories, and should not therefore be confused. God may be revealed in the things that have been made, but it does not follow that the discernment of this truth is achievable by unaided reason alone.

Towards a Theology of Nature

What is the point of all this? The doctrine of creation is that which provides a common foundation for all the human enterprises we call culture — not just theology, but science, politics, ethics, and art as well. In the high Middle Ages the foundation was provided by theology, but not by a theology of revelation. More specifically, it can be said that the framework for culture was provided more by Aristotelian-Platonic formalities than by a theology of creation. It seems clear that one of the reasons for the Scotist-Ockhamist rejection of their philosophical past was that they rejected the enterprise of basing Christian thought on a pagan philosophy. The outcome was, as we have seen, on the one hand, the rise of the dominating aspect of modern culture we call science, with its immense benefits and threats; and on the other, the rise of those aspects of culture that set themselves in direct opposition to revealed Christianity. That schizophrenic development underlies the apparent fragmentation, even dissolution, that threatens late modern culture. In the rest of this essay, I shall explore two major dimensions of the question raised by the historical development.

The first concerns what can generally be called a theology of nature: an account of what things naturally are, by virtue of their createdness. In

13. Though the link lived on in the philosophy of mechanism, the fact that that was even more disastrous for theology can only lead us to be grateful for the requirement that we think things out anew.

the Middle Ages this was generally provided, as we have seen, by what we can call the Platonic-Aristotelian synthesis. In the modern West, it was provided by what is now called foundationalism, the common foundations supposedly provided by reason and science. With the loss of foundationalism, we lose the common framework within which our culture was ordered and our moral difficulties approached. Like the medieval, the modern enterprise has collapsed, or is collapsing, under the weight of its own inadequacies. That is the truth in antifoundationalism. But its danger is in its loss of any framework for the ordering of culture — the fragmentation that is the concern of so much modern thought.

The aspect of the doctrine of creation that concerns us is its function in the establishment of universal structures of meaning. According to this, the world is made in such a way that there is at least potential correspondence between the way that it is and the way that human reason and culture may come to be. Positively, it can be argued that science as an enterprise of discovery is grounded in the doctrine of creation, and it indeed appears to be the case that without it what we call science would not have come to be. Negatively, we can say that certain possibilities are ruled out: for example, the hypothesis entertained in some science fiction that there might appear in our experience beings so alien that we could not understand them. The world is diverse, but not that diverse. It has the same structures of being and rationality everywhere. They can be misused, distorted, and the source of immense evils — as preachers of ecological doom are making all too apparent. But they are still there. "Laws which never shall be broken/for their guidance he has made." There is something to be said even for that rather deistic, foundationalist, hymn.

But let me develop rather the positive side of things, that revealed by modern science. Science could not come to be until it came to be believed that the structure of material reality, the world presented to the mind through the senses, was intelligible in its contingent relations. That is, in my view, the inescapable discovery of recent historical and conceptual studies. Without the doctrine of creation out of nothing, which affirmed the rationality, contingency, and nondivinity of the material world, the rational and experimental techniques that have brought such immense enrichment of human culture simply would not have been. But apart from revelation, biblical revelation, that could not have taken place. The doctrine of creation out of nothing, which teaches both the sheer freedom of God in creation and the distinction between God and everything that is created, does not appear to have been propounded outside those whose thinking was shaped by the biblical tradition. Everywhere else the eternity and at least sharing in divinity of the universe have been taught.

That leads me into an apparent circle. The doctrine of revelation depends upon the doctrine of creation, for it follows from its affirmation of the reality and meaningfulness, both in itself and to the human mind, of the world as God's world. Yet the doctrine of creation is itself the product of revelation for, I am claiming, without revelation we should not have a doctrine of creation. Is the circle a vicious one? Not, it appears to me, if one important point is made. In making it, I share the concerns of the intratextualists and postmoderns who claim that we are unable to gain an absolutely and objective transcendent perspective upon our world, but are in *certain respects* limited to our historical and conceptual situation. The solution is to realize that the two doctrines, of creation and revelation, are to be understood at different levels. The doctrine of creation is a material teaching, which, if we are orthodox Christians, we have come to hold, not irrationally, but not on the basis of autonomous reason either. The doctrine of revelation tells us where the belief in creation has come from: that is to say, it gives some reasons for holding beliefs that cannot be discovered by ourselves. That is the whole point of a doctrine of revelation, which is what it is precisely by virtue of the fact that by it we are taught what otherwise we could not know.[14] It is therefore a second-order doctrine, in contradiction of the recent tendency — for example, in Barth — to make revelation, or its equivalent, a first-order doctrine, and to relegate the material doctrines, like those of Nicaea, to being second order.[15] The doctrine of revelation tells us that we cannot discover certain things unless we are taught them.

The outcome of the argument so far as the material content of theology is concerned is that there is an immense difference between a theology

14. Thus the doctrine should not be used, as Thiemann has rightly argued, to cross an otherwise unbridgeable epistemological gap. Rather, its employment presupposes that a gap has already been bridged, so that the justification of revelation, such as it is, can be made only *a posteriori*.

15. I am here in fundamental disagreement with George Lindbeck, *The Nature of Doctrine: Religion and Theology in a Postliberal Age* (London: SPCK, 1984), e.g., p. 94. Enlightenment-led discussions of the nature of doctrine — that is to say, discussions that make epistemology the material center, even if they want to deny "epistemology" — make discussions of method primary, those of content secondary. But what is this except to repeat the Kantian and foundationalist error that epistemology is prior to the practice of a discipline? Recall Barth's report of Hegel's anti-Kantianism: "It was in him to ridicule the demand for a theory of knowledge by saying that there was as much sense in it as the demand of the Gascon who did not want to go into the water before he could swim. The interests of the theory of knowledge, he said, were best served in the act of a truly rational knowledge." Karl Barth, *Protestant Theology in the Nineteenth Century: Its Background and History*, tr. B. Cozens and J. Bowden (London: SCM Press, 1972), p. 393.

of nature and a natural theology. A theology of nature is the gift of biblical revelation, for it teaches us that the unity of things is upheld neither by the formal causality of the Greeks nor by the supposed omnipotence of human reason, but by the incarnate Lord whose power was exercised in the power of the Spirit and in weakness. It is because we have a theology of revelation that we can look for the glory of God in the things that have been made. This can be illustrated from a recent book on the theology and science of Michael Faraday. In it Geoffrey Cantor shows that it was Faraday's biblicism that drove his science. Particularly relevant was his belief in the authority of the Book of Genesis:

> Faraday conceived the laws of physics and chemistry as willed by God at the Creation. Moreover, the world manifests the aim of its designer. Secondly, since God created a perfect system both matter and 'force' are conserved and the system is self-sustaining.[16]

But there are more subtle theological influences than that. The doctrine of the Trinity formed a matrix for Faraday's thought, for his conception of the diversity and unity of the world drew on trinitarian conceptuality:

> The clear echo of the Christian tri-unity suggests both that the individual powers are the outward symbols of the invisible Godhead. . . . [W]hile there is great diversity in nature's appearances, this diversity is the result of a few simple laws cooperating.[17]

Here we have a theology of nature — the title of this chapter in Cantor's study — that is derived from revelation. Conceptions of unity and diversity derive from revelation. There is plurality, but not absolute plurality. Where then does that leave us in the quest for a concept of general revelation? That will be the subject of the next section.

General Revelation and Natural Theology

Just as in the previous section a distinction was drawn between a theology of nature and a natural theology, in this one I shall seek to distinguish between general revelation and natural theology. The first move is to un-

---

16. Geoffrey Cantor, *Michael Faraday: Sandemanian and Scientist. A Study of Science and Religion in the Nineteenth Century* (London: Macmillan, 1991), p. 168.
17. Cantor, p. 172.

dermine further the view that the question of general revelation is the same as the question of natural theology. As Calvin argued, there can be a general revelation that is ignored through human blindness and capacity for the creation of idols. The creation may reveal the glory of God, but "not one in a hundred" recognizes it for what it truly is. There has, then, to be a distinction between a general revelation in nature, which is indeed there, and the human capacity to appropriate it. The need for what is called special revelation is that, for various reasons, we often do not see what is there before our eyes. We may be looking for the wrong things, or more likely the right things in the wrong way, or partially in the wrong way. That is the point of Calvin's view that without the Bible as a pair of spectacles, we are unlikely to be able to recognize general revelation for what it is. The doctrine of general revelation is not therefore something that operates in parallel with biblical revelation, but is derived from it.

Given that, in what ways might we suppose that God's eternal power and deity are revealed in the things that have been made? A number of suggestions can be made. To begin with a general point, may we not say that the world reveals the glory of God because it is creation: that its contingent patterns of being have their own intrinsic rationality; that is to say, they reveal the hand of the creator because of what they are in themselves, not because they are routes to proving the existence of God?[18] Thus the world reveals its maker not because it is continuous with God, but because it is distinct, different even. Here of relevance is the point I owe to a colleague that for Calvin creation is a semiotic system: of interest not in what it means as pointing to God, but in what it means in itself. Or rather, it is as a system whose intrinsic, not extrinsic, rationality is revelatory of the one who made it. Central is the fact that the world is rational at all.

Then there is a second point, though it is related to the first. The world reveals the being of God by virtue of its capacity to be a framework for culture, that is to say, for all the varieties of human thought, action, and art that take place within it. The fact that there can be culture is a mark of the world's createdness: "God saw all that he had made, and behold, it was very good." In a sense, what I am suggesting is that secular features of the world's being are as relevant to our concerns as those that are apparently religious: good art as much as "religious" art. Those things that are discontinuous from the divine

18. Another way of putting this would be to say that the creation reveals the creator not by virtue of formal patterns of rationality indicating some continuity between the world and God, but by developments of the implications of the doctrine of the univocity of the concept of being.

speak the power and deity of God by virtue of what they are. Art is a case in point. For Barth, Mozart proved that all creation praised its maker not because he was trying to prove something, to make points — that is the way of natural theology — but because he simply allowed the music to do its own work. Mozart's *revelatory* quality for Barth was that he does not try to teach, but simply to play, and it is as such that he teaches us that all creation is perfect and praises its maker.[19] The world is thus the source of general revelation because of the beauty, both natural and cultural, that can and does exist within it.

The third and in some ways crucial point arises from the illustration from the work of Faraday, which suggests that not the patterns of Platonic formality or of Aristotelian causality but of trinitarian relationality offer possibilities for drawing analogies between the being of God and that of the world. The world reveals the hand that made it in the remarkable combination of unity and diversity, of relationality and particularity, that it manifests, marks that can be recognized by their analogy to the unity and diversity of the triune God. This is the point of Professor T. F. Torrance's suggestion that we look for parallel rationalities. The revelation of the creator is to be found in the fact that creator and creation represent parallel or analogous structures of rationality.[20] Revelation suggests ways of seeing parallels between uncreated and created rationality, but we need not be too anxious about finding a way between them. God has done that already in Christ.

In that sense, we do not need to be foundationalist, for the reason that there is no other foundation laid for our faith than Jesus Christ our Lord, the one in whom the creation holds together. As we have seen, that is not to evade the challenges of rationality, but to establish them on their proper basis: not on impersonal Platonic-Aristotelian structures, but on the free personal relation of God to the world through his Son and Spirit. It is the trinitarian formulation of a doctrine of creation that allows God to be God, the world to be the world, distinct beings and yet personally related by personal mediation as creator and creation. Equally important for our purposes, the plurality in unity of the triune revelation enables us to do justice to the diversity, richness, and openness of the world without denying its unity in relativist versions of pluralism. It is that vision that trinitarian theology has to offer the fragmented modern world.

19. Karl Barth, *Church Dogmatics*, 3/3, p. 299; and Colin Gunton, "Mozart the Theologian," *Theology* 94 (1991): 346-49.

20. T. F. Torrance, *The Ground and Grammar of Theology* (Belfast: Christian Journals, 1980), p. 100. In this "viewing together" of created and uncreated intelligibility or rationality, I would not necessarily want to speak of a transformed natural theology, it seeming preferable to maintain the distinction between that and a theology of nature.

7

Immanence and Transcendence in Trinitarian Theology

HENRI BLOCHER

*Theon oudeis heôraken pôpote; monogenés Theos ho ôn eis ton kolpon
tou Patros ekeinos exégésato.*

Immanence, transcendence, even *Trinity:* what mouth-filling words, what
bombastic abstractions! Under my title, I run the risk indeed of presumptuous, and therefore empty, jargon: *vain* talk in both senses of that term.
Hence the *blessing* I receive in the plainer language of Scripture, my only
protection against vanity. My effort will be to root what I have to say in
that language, the one that the Spirit himself has taught us (1 Cor. 2:13).

Our abstract, technical words are not even guaranteed against equiv-
ocation. "Immanent," especially, may be used in a variety of ways in theology proper. Some older divines would call *immanentia* a class of divine
attributes, opposed to the *transeuntia* or "transitive" ones: so, I read, Calov,
Quenstedt, Hollaz,[1] still followed by A. H. Strong. More relevant to our
theme, "the immanent Trinity" is the traditional phrase for the Trinity of
Father, Son, and Holy Spirit considered independently of the *economy* of
creation and redemption — God before all times, the Trinity in the *opera
ad intra.* Thus understood, the immanent Trinity is an altogether different
point from what is commonly called divine immanence. To prevent silly
stumbling at mere words, I shall rather say "the ontological Trinity" when

---

1. Karl Hase, *Hutterus redivivus, oder Dogmatik der evangelisch-lutherischen Kirche*
(Leipzig: Breitkopf & Hartel, 1848), p. 131.

referring to the Trinity of God *in se,* as distinguished from the economic Trinity.[2]

The first problem that comes to mind when we associate the thoughts of immanence, transcendence, and Trinity — at least, in our late twentieth-century situation — is precisely that of *ontology vs. economy.* Affirming immanence, in the eyes of many, amounts to professing immanent*ism,* to denying any possibility of a meaningful discourse on God *apart* from the world, *apart* from history. There seems to be a kinship, and a convergence, between the stress on immanence and the economic Trinity, on the one hand, and between the stress on transcendence and the ontological Trinity, on the other.

However, we shall have to discern that immanence in the orthodox understanding yields not an inch to immanentism. Another question, then, will arise: that of possible relationships between immanence and transcendence, *as acknowledged by evangelical theology,* and the Trinity.

All this we shall attempt in the following order: first, to clarify and to "flesh out" with biblical help the main notions involved, while avowing presuppositions and methodological preferences; second, to look into the ontology *vs.* economy debate; finally, to consider how trinitarian truth may relate to the twin attributes — not polar opposites — immanence and transcendence.

Starting Blocks

Since, obviously, setting forth and defending the doctrine of the Trinity would far exceed the scope of this paper, I shall be excused, hopefully, if I merely confess my *credo* in the form of a few sentences:

(a) The classic doctrine of the Trinity, the Church dogma as endorsed by the magisterial sixteenth-century Reformation and as formulated, for instance, in the *quicumque vult,* can and must be maintained.

(b) Its normative power, final authority, flows from its agreement with Scripture. Here also the *Sola Scriptura, Sola et tota Scriptura,* provides the valid foundation.

I am so bold as to differ from most prestigious theologians today. Wolfhart Pannenberg (who does not appear to have retracted his *Entpositivierung* motto, in spite of milder tones) argues at some length against the

2. According to Pannenberg, the formal distinction between economic and essential Trinity can be traced back to Joh. Urlsperger, 1769-74 and 1777. Wolfhart Pannenberg, *Systematische Theologie,* vol. 1 (Göttingen: Vandenhoeck & Ruprecht, 1988), p. 317 n. 112.

older Protestant conviction that the Trinity may be proven from Scripture: the data, in his view, are too meager *(schmal),* unclear, ambiguous, to be used as a basis for certainty.[3] Eberhard Jüngel, who has shown a notable respect for biblical authority, will not grant the sufficiency of a New Testament foundation.[4] Unashamed, however, I dare claim that the doctrine of the Trinity is present in the texts: unsystematized, in nontechnical language as most other doctrines are, but with no less certainty. It is not only latent and implicit, but we can spot here and there, mostly in the Johannine corpus, distinct sights of thematization.

Apart from such scriptural grounds, I doubt the possibility of ever affirming, with any rigor, the divine Trinity, at any rate the ontological Trinity. It may not be inferred from pure "event." To receive the most marvelous mystery, we need the teaching of God himself; to believe the unbelievable revelation, we need his word and signature!

(c) Western tradition, we should acknowledge, has overprivileged unity of essence and understressed the threeness of God, as Colin Gunton, even more brilliantly than others, has shown in the case of St. Augustine.[5] As one marked, in his younger years, by Leonard Hodgson's epoch-making monograph, I am in sympathy with this critique. I have long taken pains to avoid any division and isolation of the treatise *De Deo uno* from *De Deo trino.* But I would add a few comments relating to the present state of the question.

I have to confess some mixed feelings when I hear the praise currently lavished on the Greek, especially Cappadocian, Fathers. Did not even the great Basil slip into embarrassing turns of phrases that could suggest a merely *generic* unity of the Three? Is it possible to deny the presence of a *subordinationist* strain in the trinitarian theology of the fourth-century giants? I cannot but concur with Pannenberg's diagnosis of these weaknesses.[6]

St. Augustine's difficulty, it seems, centered on the distinction between *relative* and *relational:* his precious discernment was that of the *relations* as establishing difference without impairing unity — but he tended to move from this discovery to a conclusion of *relativity* as implying second-ranking

3. Pannenberg, *Systematische Theologie,* pp. 293, 295, 327ff.; at p. 295, Pannenberg quotes Wiles saying that we cannot rely on scriptural statements as the Fathers did, and in n. 45, he agrees that we can no longer accept the idea of a "propositional revelation."

4. Eberhard Jüngel, *Dieu, mystère du monde. Fondement de la théologie du Crucifié dans le débat entre théisme et athéisme,* vol. 2, tr. into French by Horst Homburg (Paris: Cerf, 1983), pp. 203-4 (corresponds to pp. 480-81 in the original German, 3d ed.).

5. Colin Gunton, "Augustine, the Trinity and the Theological Crisis of the West," *Scottish Journal of Theology* 43 (1990): 33-58.

6. Pannenberg, *Systematische Theologie,* pp. 298, 304.

status, an unfortunate step. Platonic hyperrealism made him wary of affirming three "persons" because "personhood," then, as a real essence, would appear to exist three times, and to be a mere generic bond between Father, Son, and Spirit. He was influenced, together with the whole tradition, by the Neoplatonic worship of the One, but we should not ignore the complexity of both the factors and the stakes. The Western, or Latin, starting point in the *one essence of deity* already emerges in Tertullian's account of the Trinity, in a different, philosophical environment. The most powerful constraint was, simply, *biblical* monotheism! How shall we meet the challenge of Judaism and of Islam if we relax the rigor of the great Witness (*'ēd*): *Shema' Yisraēl* . . . (Deut. 6:4)? The trend toward "social" views of the Trinity looks dangerously unaware of the gravity of tritheism:[7] assigning to the Three a generic or corporative unity equals tritheism, it *is* tritheism!

When reviewing our dogmatic heritage, we should take note of André Malet's remarkable piece of scholarship, on *Person and Love in St Thomas Aquinas' Trinitarian Theology*.[8] Contrary to common opinion, he argues powerfully that St. Thomas made up for the deficiencies in the Augustinian treatment, that he emphasized the threeness at least as strongly as the Greek Fathers had done.

(d) Critics often indulge in stiff and hardened readings of traditional doctrine in order to justify discarding it. One may legitimately use the concepts of *hupostasis* (person), relation, *opus,* in a flexible, analogical way. It can be done without falling into the Charybdis of agnosticism (including Neoplatonic *apophasis, nescientia,* negative theology) nor into the Scylla of a wooden, anthropomorphic representation. God *incomprehensible,* yet God *intelligible* by means of his revelation: both are vital. John Frame strikes a fine balance when he analyzes the limitations that our finiteness entails for our knowledge of God.[9] In Jacques Maritain's words, our concepts "acknowledge themselves as powerless to enclose or to fence the reality they refer to," but "they yield for us, as they kneel before him, the knowledge of God."[10] "We see — yet in a mirror, *en ainigmati*" (1 Cor. 13:12): both parts of the statement are vital.

---

7. Symptomatic in this regard would be the article by Cornelius Plantinga, Jr., "The Threeness/Oneness Problem of the Trinity," *Calvin Theological Journal* 23 (1988): 37-53.

8. André Malet, *Personne et amour dans la théologie trinitaire de saint Thomas d'Aquin* (Paris: Jules Vrin, 1956); when he wrote this book, A. Malet held a chair at the Institut Catholique, Paris; he later became a Bultmannian and left the Roman Catholic Church.

9. John Frame, *The Doctrine of the Knowledge of God* (Phillipsburg, NJ: Presbyterian & Reformed, 1987), pp. 20-39.

10. Jacques Maritain, *Les Degrés du savoir,* as quoted by Charles Journet, *Connaissance et inconnaissance de Dieu* (Paris: Egloff, 1943), p. 52 n. 1.

If our faith, while *quaerens intellectum,* remembers that God remains beyond human understanding, our faith reflects on God's *transcendence.* Transcendence, agreeing with etymology, means "beyondness," rising and lying above — transcendence is trans*a*scendence, Lévinas writes[11] — surpassing excellence.

Transcendence is a connotation we may overhear in such divine names as *'ēl* and *Shadday* in the Old Testament. In ordinary contexts, at least, *YHWH,* more strongly *YHWH sebaōt* (LORD of the heavenly hosts, both angels and stars) would suggest it. *'elyōn,* Most High, could be specialized in that direction, as the metaphor of height is akin to the idea of transcendence. Isaiah 57:15, that jewel of prophetic preaching, expresses it together with the paradox of merciful condescension, and the polemical oratory of 40:12ff. extols the Lord's immeasurable superiority, incomparable power, unfathomable intelligence. The symbolism of heaven, throughout the Bible, reinforces the theme: adding to distance all-encompassing, *umgreifende,* depth and breadth.

The lexical family of *PL',* in Old Testament Hebrew, seems most precisely to express the concept of transcendence. It is used to suggest what eludes human grasp: Why do you ask my name? It is *pēlī,* beyond a mortal's comprehension (Judg. 13:18; cf. Gen. 32:29; 18:14 uses the same root). In the New Testament, *hyperbolē* could be rendered "transcendence" in 2 Corinthians 4:7: We hold this treasure in earthen vessels in order that the transcendence of the Power be ascribed to God and not to us.

A significant metaphorical cluster relates to the sense of sight. God dwells in inaccessible light (1 Tim. 6:16: What a proclamation of transcendence!). No man can see him and live — his face shall not be seen — no man has ever seen God (Exod. 33:20, 23; John 1:18). Hence the dark clouds in which the Lord of the theophanic storm wraps himself (Ps. 18:12), and the darkness of Sinai (Deut. 4:11; 5:22). Hence Solomon's dictum: "The Lord has said that he would dwell in the thick darkness" (1 Kings 8:12) and the maxim on God's glory in concealing a matter (Prov. 25:2). Mystics seized upon these symbols to evoke divine transcendence, loaded with Neoplatonic additions: "the Cloud of Unknowing" (fourteenth century), *la noche oscura* of St. John of the Cross (remember the refrain of his poem of "the hidden fount": *aunque es de noche . . .*).

As we receive biblical instruction, we should note the context of divine transcendence, close to exaltation, majesty, holiness, and discern its distinctive shade of meaning. John Frame happily stresses the association with

11. Emmanuel Lévinas, *Totalité et Infini. Essai sur l'extériorité* (Pocket ed. *s.l.:* Kluwer Academic, 1990 [1st ed., The Hague: Martinus Nijhoff, 1971]), p. 24.

lordship, or, as he says, covenant headship, "control and authority"[12] (maybe a less felicitous choice of terms); this is sounder than speculation about infinity, which is no frequent theme in Scripture. It reminds us helpfully of the main connections of the biblical idea. Yet, the proper nuance of transcendence remains hidden in the shadow of the massive lordship theme. We should not confuse transcendence with reign. It also implies *otherness*, the absolute nonsymmetry between the Creator and everything that has come to be, *panta ha gegonen* (John 1:3), and the movement of going beyond. . . . St. Anselm's "negative name" for God, *Quo majus cogitari nequit*, better expresses his transcendence. Or the Muslim *Allahu akhbar!* It is a comparative form, we are told: God is great*er*.

Again, transcendence differs from majesty, we are wont to say, as Ezekiel's *merkaba* differs from Isaiah's seraphic one in the Temple. The visions do correspond and agree, but observe the nuances! The otherness, the unnatural character, of Ezekiel's complex machinery; the escalation up to super-superlative-superlativity; and then, *quo majus cogitari nequit*, high above, seated on a hypercosmic throne, "the likeness, as the appearance of a man"! The likeness means that the biblical Lord transcends even transcendence, that is, all our imaginings of transcendence. Which also is the message of Hosea 11:9: "I will not execute my fierce anger . . . for I am God, and not man, the Holy One in your midst" (NASV rendering).

"Immanence," the other term to introduce, does not belong to the treasury of classical Latin. The Scholastics coined the word *immanens* for actions that remain within the agent, as opposed to transitive action, *exiens* or *transiens*; Spinoza remained faithful to this use: *Deus ergo est omnium rerum causa immanens, non vero transiens* (*Ethics*, I,18)[13] — which could be called *the* theorem of immanentism. Immanuel Kant calls "immanent" those principles of pure reason *(Verstand)* the use of which remains strictly within the bounds of possible experience, and these he wishes to uphold.[14] It is no secret that Kant's rejection of transcendent sources of knowledge may be considered as the fatal shunting of modern theology.

In the sense of being confined within the world, or empirical bounds, immanence would not be compatible with divine transcendence; it may not be predicated of the biblical God. The root folly of the depraved mind

12. Frame, pp. 13, 15-16.

13. André Lalande, *Vocabulaire technique et critique de la philosophie* (Paris: F. Alcan, 1932), p. 345.

14. Immanuel Kant, *Kritik der reinen Vernunft*, neuherausg. v. Raymund Schmidt (Leipzig: Felix Meiner, 1927), p. 336. I have been led to this passage by Lalande, pp. 344-45.

lies in the confusion of Creator and creature (Rom. 1:22-23). In the Spinozistic sense, immanence does imply pantheism; it cannot be affirmed without a betrayal of the Christian faith; Pius X's condemnation, in his famous encyclical *Pascendi dominici gregis* (9 September 1907), applies.[15] But the etymology of the word allows for another use of "immanence," divine immanence: it may refer to God's permanent *indwelling* of his creation; *such* an immanence belongs to the doctrine of Scripture. The one hundred thirty-ninth psalm immediately jumps to mind as one mentions immanence, with the mighty celebration of God's presence everywhere, before and behind, to both ends of the world, from the height of heaven to the bottomless deep. Already, Jacob's experience at Luz, which he called, for that reason, Bethel, led him to realize the presence of his fathers' God in the strange country of his flight. God is there.

Other data are relevant too. Psalm 139 combines the thought of God's knowledge with that of his presence: "God is there" means "God sees." This is an important biblical emphasis. The Lord is the one "who sees me," *'ēl rō'î* (Gen. 16:13), he is aware, "there is no creature hidden from his sight" (Heb. 4:13). The eyes of the Lord range throughout the earth (Zech. 4:10), they are everywhere, keeping watch over the wicked and over the good (Prov. 15:3), over all their ways (Jer. 16:17). God's presence, at the same time, sustains all creatures in existence and life: were he to withdraw, they would instantly vanish (Ps. 104; Heb. 1:3). And so, it fills the world, and every atom in the world (Jer. 23:24; Eph. 1:23 makes the same claim for the glorious Christ).

Older dogmatics used to say that God's presence in created space is not circumscriptive, as in the case of bodies, nor definitive, as in the case of created spirits, but *repletive,* filling and fulfilling.[16] For "presence" is no simple, easy, notion! Francisco Turretin(i), after he has rehearsed the various special modes of the divine presence,[17] comes to God's universal immanence, and he quotes a handy scholastic verse:

15. H. Leclere, "Immanence," in *Catholicisme, hier, aujourd'hui, demain,* vol. 5, ed. G. Jacquemet (Paris: Letouzey & Ané, 1963), p. 1298.

16. Charles Hodge, *Systematic Theology,* vol. 1 (Grand Rapids: Eerdmans, 1986 repr.), p. 384.

17. Franciscus Turretinus, *Institutio theologiae elencticae,* vol. 1 (New York: Robert Garter, 1847 repr.), p. 178. His summary of the special modes, although not our topic, nor his in the section, is worth quoting in full: "Non quaeritur de variis praesentia divinae specialis modis, secundum quod dicitur esse, *In Christo* per unionem hypostaticam et Deitatis plenitudinem, Col. ii.9. *In Coelo* per gloriam, 1 Reg. viii.27. *In Ecclesia* per gratiam: Ezec. xlviii.35; quae rursus, vel est *praesentia symbolica,* quando sub aliquo visibili symbolo se fidelibus patefecit, ut Mosi in Rubo, populo in Columna nubis, Patribus sub forma Angelorum et hominum; vel *praesentia sacramentalis* et mystica, quum sub signis et elementis gratiam suam

Enter, praesenter Deus est, et ubique potenter.

The threefold division answers to the creaturely need of God as the onto-logical ground, the reference point of all knowledge, and the source of all power.[18] It might be related to Acts 17:28: We *live* by his sustaining power (power to live and love); in him we *move* — our every move known, measured, determined, interpreted, of him; and we *have our being*.

Do we perceive the semantic shade of immanence? Divine immanence is *pervasive* presence, granted to galaxies down to the last particle of matter. Divine immanence is inhabitation, *indwelling* presence: God is "at home" in the world; he is not present as a visitor in a foreign territory — all these things, which his hand has made, are his (Isa. 66:1-2); the earth is the Lord's greater temple, resounding in every corner with his praise (Ps. 29:9).

Such an immanence does not impugn transcendence. Rather, it im-plies transcendence, and conversely.[19] The pervasive and indwelling pres-ence, *praesentia* with the Latin connotations of power and command, in-volves no confusion with created being: it *expresses* the other side of transcendence. Both transcendence and immanence tell of the divine *more*, and *beyond*, the true *akhbar*. St. Augustine had his own unsurpassed way of confessing it: *Tu autem eras interior intimo meo et superior summo meo* — Thou wast more deeply within myself than my innermost part, and higher than the highest part of my being.[20]

The Noncorrelative God

Our conviction that an essential solidarity binds immanence and transcen-dence together cannot blind us to the fact that they *seem* to crystallize antagonistic truths; and there is a real tension when immanence takes on immanentistic overtones. The one spells out God's aloofness from the world and the other his involvement within it, the one suggests God's union with created being and the other his infinite difference remaining. Many theo-logians, in order to accommodate for both, have been attracted to a trini-tarian model.

---

nobis obsignat et exhibet; vel *praesentia spiritualis* et vivifica, quum per spiritum habitat in cordibus fidelium."

18. Turretinus, p. 178; Hodge, p. 384.

19. Leclere, p. 1297.

20. St. Augustine, *The Confessions* 3.6.11.

Tillich's courage to be . . . Tillich prompts one to offer a glaring illustration of such an exploitation of the doctrine of the Trinity. The German-American theologian openly interprets the church dogma as the pregnant symbol of the dialectical relationship between being-itself and concrete finite beings: "Trinitarian monotheism is not a matter of the number three. It is a qualitative and not a quantitative characterization of God. It is an attempt to speak of the living God, the God in whom the ultimate and the concrete are united."[21] It satisfies the double pull of monism and dualism. Being-itself is immanent, since being-itself does not "exist," but is the power of being *in* all beings; yet being-itself, as such, transcends all finite beings. In Tillich's favorite phrases, being-itself is both the Ground and the Abyss of all beings, *Grund* and *Abgrund,* maybe with the Boehmian twist, *Urgrund* and *Ungrund.* The Trinity, as it incorporates plurality within the One, and as it unites the Absolute God and a concrete finite man, signifies the dialectics of being. "The finite is posited as finite within the process of the divine life, but it is reunited with the infinite within the same process";[22] thus, "the trinitarian principles are moments within the process of the divine life," the abyss, the logos, and their actual-ization.[23]

In more guarded ways, a similar tendency prevailed among the theo-logical generation of the sixties — theologians who rose to prominence and fame during that decade. Moltmann is probably the best known among them, and Jüngel the one who enjoys the highest academic prestige. New was the rejection of "theism" and indulgence in "panentheistic" talk; strong was the interest in the Trinity, but this with unmistakably Hegelian features: the Trinity interpreted as the "history of God" and based on the *man* Jesus, Jesus *qua* man as the second Person. More precisely, the *crucified* Jesus: this approach claimed to side with Luther's *theologia crucis* over against theism (suspected to be a theology of glory), and, thus, to solve the theodicy problem after Auschwitz.

Elements in Barth and Bonhoeffer did pave the way for this move, as Jüngel has brought to light. An important influence was the Heideggerian scorn poured on "ontotheology." Generally speaking, the antimetaphysical, anti-*Greek* climate of opinion entailed disfavor for the Christology and the Triadology of the councils. The underlying factor, the most potent of all in

---

21. Paul Tillich, *Systematic Theology,* vol. 1 (Chicago: University of Chicago Press, 1951), p. 228.

22. Tillich, p. 251.

23. Tillich, p. 250.

my estimate, was the widespread distrust in the older method of theology — building upon the *dicta Dei, dicta a Deo*, of Scripture.[24] The conclusion of critical analysis often was, as mentioned earlier, that the biblical foundation could not bear such a heavy monument as trinitarian dogma; but even if it were able to support the grand construction, that way of theologizing would have to be rejected, for the Trinity should be derived from the core of the Christian faith, from the central event of Christian proclamation.

There is a subtler ambiguity, not to say an added oddity, in Pannenberg's case. Although he may reprove "the view of the one divine being as Person in the sense of self-consciousness as *the heresy of Christian theism*,"[25] sharp words indeed, the Munich systematician wishes to uphold monotheism: he boldly proclaims the Trinity, according to the confession of the ancient church, as "the Christian form of monotheism" and "the condition of a thorough-going monotheism" and vigorously chides J. Moltmann for denying it.[26] He lucidly realizes that Christian theology would crumble down without an immanent, ontological Trinity.[27] On the other hand, he charges "the classical doctrine of the Trinity" with hypostatizing its God at a prehistorical stage and of making him historical "only in a secondary way";[28] the resurrection of Jesus, he adds, is "constitutive for the deity of the Father as it is for the divine sonship of Jesus."[29] The same constitutive role he attributes to the self-differentiation of Jesus from the Father, of Jesus *as man* from the Father *as God* (emphasis his!), that Jesus "receives his deity from the Father in the act of self-differentiation" and the Father's "own deity depends on the Son."[30] The man Jesus' actions

24. See Jüngel, vol. 1, pp. 242ff. (no infallible jurisdiction; corresponds to pp. 210ff. in the original); for Pannenberg, see n. 3 above.

25. Wolfhart Pannenberg, "Die Subjektivitaet Gottes und die Trinitaetslehre. Ein Beitrag zur Beziehung zwischen Karl Barth und der Philosophie Hegels," *Kerygma und Dogma* 23 (1977): 39.

26. Pannenberg, "Die Subjektivitaet," pp. 39-40 n. 34. Also *Systematische Theologie*, p. 363.

27. Roger E. Olson, "Wolfhart Pannenberg's Doctrine of the Trinity," *Scottish Journal of Theology* 43 (1990): 196; I have found Olson's synthesis most helpful.

28. Wolfhart Pannenberg, "Der Gott der Geschichte. Der trinitarische Gott und die Wahrheit der Geschichte," *Kerygma und Dogma* 23 (1977): 87.

29. Pannenberg, "Der Gott der Geschichte," p. 87.

30. Pannenberg, *Systematische Theologie*, pp. 337-38, 340 (the Father's "eigene Gottheit nun vom Sohn abhängt"); at pp. 336-37, Pannenberg mentions the orthodox treatment (by Hollaz) of Jesus' words of self-differentiation from God: Jesus speaks only as man; Pannenberg replies that this is not valid on the basis of orthodox Christology, since Jesus speaks of his person, not of his human nature. I consider Pannenberg to be mistaken here: things are

(and passions) seem to come first, and their outcome, then, to be eternal-ized. The Trinity's dependence on history offers also a key to theodicy, since the incorporation of a created being confers an ultimate consistency to creaturely life: "The difference between the Father as Creator and the Son and the Spirit, through whom only his creation will reach consummation, makes room also, together with the autonomy of the creature, for the possibility of a perversion of its order."[31] Stakes are high on both sides!

Pannenberg is not blind to the difficulty. While he does not hide his sympathy with Jüngel's, Moltmann's, and Jenson's stress on the "dependence of the Father's deity on the course of history,"[32] he also heeds Walter Kasper's warning against the absorption of the immanent Trinity into economy. He therefore expressly rules out that "the trinitarian God be the result of history, that he should only attain his reality in eschatological consummation."[33] Does he mean, then, that his previous statements that suggested such a meaning are valid only *quoad nos*, as far as our subjective grasp of the truth is concerned? We could interpret him in this way, as he focuses on the definitive *demonstration* of God's deity *(endgültig erwiesen sein wird)*, on the fact that otherwise it would be "unthinkable." Yet, he does not call the End the mere manifestation of God's eternal truth: he calls it "the locus of the decision." He immediately comes back to "the dependence of [God's] existence on the eschatological consummation of his Reign." Although he maintains divine eternity (implying the ontological Trinity), he offers as the solution that "the constitutive significance of eschatological consummation for the very eternity of God be taken into account in the understanding of this eternity."[34] Pannenberg's conscious effort aims at combining what others would consider to be incompatible theses: "the eternal self-identity of God and the disputability of his truth in the historical process, as well as the decision on his truth by means of the consummation of history."[35] A double pull quite typical of Pannenberg's style![36]

---

predicated of the person by virtue of the natures he possesses, and some things may be said of the person by virtue of one of his natures only.

31. Pannenberg, "Der Gott der Geschichte," p. 90: "Die Differenz des Vaters als des Schöpfers von Sohn und Geist, durch die seine Schöpfung erst vollendet werden kann, gibt nun aber mit der Selbstständigkeit des Geschöpfes zugleich auch der Möglichkeit einer Verkehrung seiner Bestimmung Raum."

32. Pannenberg, *Systematische Theologie*, pp. 357-58.

33. Pannenberg, *Systematische Theologie*, p. 359.

34. Pannenberg, *Systematische Theologie*, p. 359.

35. Pannenberg, *Systematische Theologie*, p. 361.

36. Jim S. Halsey observed a similar unresolved "double pull." Jim S. Halsey, "History, Language, and Hermeneutics: The Synthesis of Wolfhart Pannenberg," *Westminster Theological Journal* 41 (1979): 269-90 (phrase used on p. 290).

Are the prospects favorable to Pannenberg's endeavor, or does it rather look like having one's cake and eating it? "At the basis of Pannenberg's claim about Jesus' eternal sonship lies a fundamental principle," Roger Olson suggests, "that God's deity *is* his lordship."[37] This is why God's deity depends on the completion of the work of Jesus and the Spirit, the historical agents of the Reign. But to identify God's being and his rule would require a rather brutal step.[38] Moreover, can such a view of deity avoid the pitfall of tritheism? Pannenberg's former student Fall Wagner, quoted and followed by R. Olson,[39] raises serious doubts. Another thought that Pannenberg obviously cherishes and that plays an important part in his theology is this: the infinite, to be truly infinite, must overcome and encompass its opposition with the finite.[40] Hence the possibility of Jesus' inclusion in the Godhead. This insight reminds us of the old Lutheran reply to the *finitum non capax infiniti* of the Reformed: yes, but *infinitum capax finiti!* However, one can question the application of this highly speculative principle: it may refute dualism and so make room for incarnation, but it does not require or justify inserting a man as such (in humble self-differentiation from God and abnegation) in the constitution of the divine being. It is no surprise if several observers feel that Pannenberg jettisons the distinction between God and his creation.[41] Ultimately, Pannenberg's proposal hinges upon his original affirmation of *ontological retroactivity*, which he introduced in his *Grundzüge Christologie:* Jesus' historical resurrection (later emphasis falls on mission and submission) is the basis or ground of his deity, but so eternally, for it works backward ontologically.[42] The older Pannenberg uses more restraint, but he does not appear to have relinquished the thought;[43]

37. Olson, pp. 188, 199.

38. Pannenberg, *Systematische Theologie,* pp. 340-41 (tries to be cautious).

39. Olson, pp. 192-93.

40. Pannenberg, "Die Subjektivität," p. 40 n. 34; "Der Gott der Geschichte," p. 89.

41. This was the uneasy feeling of several Swiss theologians at a conference with Pannenberg, according to the account of their debate, by Denis Mueller, in J. L. Leuba and C. J. Pinto de Oliveira, eds., *Hegel et la théologie contemporaine* (Neuchâtel & Paris: Delachaux & Niestlé, 1977), pp. 220.-21. Timothy Bradshaw wonders whether Pannenberg can preserve a hypostasis of creation, in the end, "to be God's partner"; Pannenberg is said to come "close to an inversion of the classical *enhypostasia,* in that a finite man is the subject of deity." Timothy Bradshaw, *Trinity and Ontology. A Comparative Study of the Theologies of Karl Barth and Wolfhart Pannenberg* (Edinburgh: Rutherford House Books, 1988), pp. 341, 356.

42. Wolfhart Pannenberg, *Esquisse d'une christologie,* tr. into French by A. Liefooghe (Paris: Cerf, 1971), pp. 164-65, 282, 391.

43. Pannenberg, *Systematische Theologie,* pp. 288 (including the rendering in Rom. 1:3-4, "eingesetzt werden"), 359-60.

he refers to the apocalyptic mind: "The fact that everything which shall be revealed in the end is already present in the hidden world of God corresponds to a general rule of apocalyptic representation."[44] But whence the authority of apocalyptic representations? Ontological retroactivity offers a most glaring example of *metabasis eis allo genos:* what is meaningful in the realm of law (it may apply to past affairs insofar as present and future consequences are in view) is transferred to being; and time is treated as space, with moves possible in all directions! We confess how baffled we feel to register reactions so mild to that gem in "teratologics."[45] There are great experts in straining out gnats and swallowing . . . chimeras.

We may be forgiven for asking a naive question. For all their artful and learned presentation, whether in the more "user-friendly" version of Moltmann or the more sophisticated one of Jüngel, or through the tensions and twists of Pannenberg, would any of these post-Hegelian constructions of the Trinity lead readers to believe in a One God, Father, Son, and Holy Spirit, apart from the memory of the church dogma? They draw their persuasive power from the compromise between external continuity with theological tradition, including the use of trinitarian formulae, and philosophical concordance with the *Zeitgeist.* Jüngel, for instance, may appear to be more restrained and sensitive than his peers if, indeed, he has peers; yet, one easily perceives his underlying conviction that we *cannot* think but through Descartes, Hegel, and Heidegger. He valiantly strives to go *beyond* them, but discarding their contribution is no live option; in other words, there can be no *radical* critique of the modern philosophical stance.

The wide gulf, or "ugly ditch," that lies between orthodox doctrine and the new trinities should not be minimized. It is simply not the case that they could pass for updated renderings of the old dogma. In spite of Jüngel's homage to the Fathers, to the Reformers,[46] in spite of Pannenberg's *Grundlichkeit* on issues of historical theology, they differ deeply in their foundation, elaboration, and import.

Is the meaning of what is seemingly maintained truly preserved? The Son's preexistence becomes that of the *man* Jesus — not the *logos asarkos,* perish the thought![47] — either in the equivocal sense of predestination,

44. Pannenberg, *Systematische Theologie*, p. 289.

45. Walter Kasper senses the weakness of Pannenberg's key argument, but he is satisfied with a mild "infelicitous" comment. Walter Kasper, *Jésus le Christ,* tr. into French by J. Desigaux and A. Liefooghe (Paris: Cerf, 1976), p. 247n. Jüngel agrees with Pannenberg, in a footnote. Jüngel, vol. 2, p. 223 n. 175 (German: p. 497).

46. Jüngel, vol. 1, p. 287 (German: p. 249).

47. Jüngel, vol. 1, p. 119 (German: p. 103).

which is no existence except by abuse of words,[48] or by virtue of ontological retroactivity. *Sonship* itself is weakened to mean intimacy, election, or approval on God's part, obedience and self-denial on Jesus' part.[49] It follows that the *gift* of the Son by the Father becomes a rather hollow form of speech: there is no Father and no Son, in true theological order, prior to the giving; if God identifies himself with that faithful man ("identifies" — a conveniently ambiguous term), it is not the same as if he gives his preexistent, eternal Son, first that he may become a man, and then as the sacrificial victim. Where is the *freedom of grace* if God owes his full self-identity to the historical event of the cross and the resurrection? Our theologians are not unaware of the difficulty, but can only move round it.[50] Are we even in a position still to speak of a historical event? History is no longer treated as history when it is transmuted into a manipulation of concepts, a dialectics of essences. With the professed intention of involving metaphysics in history, one loses history in metaphysics.[51] The significant phrase here is Hegel's "speculative Good Friday":[52] the speculative Good Friday amounts to the loss of the real Good Friday. And so, instead of the historical work of atonement through the ransom of blood and the satisfaction of justice, we read about being and nonbeing, nonbeing incorporated into being, nonbeing thereby overcome by being — how illuminating such a language compared with that of the Bible! History, I plead, requires a prior foundation in being, a metaphysical framework in which, and metaphysical subjects for whom, events can happen. Mixing the two ruins both.

One often hears the insinuation that the only alternative to trinities of Hegelian descent is the pagan god of ontotheology, the lifeless abstraction of Greek rationalism. Against such an oversimplification, I would claim:

48. Pannenberg attributes fluid ideas to the New Testament Christians: the reflection, rather, of modern conceptions. Pannenberg, *Systematische Theologie*, p. 289.

49. Pannenberg does not repeat his *Grundzuege* attacks against the two natures and tries to find the "root" in the two "aspects" of Jesus' person (self-denying man). Pannenberg, *Systematische Theologie*, p. 338. Jüngel, also, speaks in rather respectful terms, but it does not amount to more than formal softening of a clear denial. Jüngel, vol. 2, p. 169 n. 186 (German: p. 450).

50. Jüngel, vol. 1, pp. 344-45 (German: p. 300); Pannenberg, *Systematische Theologie*, pp. 359ff.

51. Oliver O'Donovan offers an argument akin to our point: "When history is made the categorical matrix for all meaning and value, it cannot then be taken seriously as history. A story has to be a story about something; but when everything is story there is nothing for story to be about." Oliver O'Donovan, *Resurrection and Moral Order: An Outline for Evangelical Ethics* (Leicester: Inter-Varsity Press, 1986), p. 60.

52. (Respectfully) quoted by Jüngel, vol. 1, pp. 116, 120 (German: pp. 101, 104).

tertium datur. And this other view is the biblical one. Scripture itself witnesses loud and clear to the living God as immutable and independent.[53] The two-natures Christological scheme emerges at several junctures in the New Testament.[54] It may even play a determinative role in theological argument: the crowning privilege, in Paul's well-constructed list of the advantages of Israel (Rom. 9:1-5), is to provide the stock from which, as far as his human nature is concerned *(to karta sarka),* comes the one who is God over all — no higher privilege can be thought of for a fleshly community as such. The Epistle to the Hebrews (chs. 1–2) establishes the Son's superiority, as the mediator, over the angels, on the basis, first, of his deity and, then, of his humanity: the God-man, both higher and lower than the angels, is the bridge unsurpassed between the Father and the children of flesh and blood. The prologue of the fourth Gospel draws the concept of incarnation (and gives more than hints of an interest in the ontological grounds of economy). These, and other passages, have already strong Chalcedonian implications, and give the lie to the Hegelian axiom about the cross: "Dies not a man but the divine."[55]

Schelling, his fellow student of the younger years at the Tübingen *Stift,* realized that Hegel robbed his God of all true transcendence.[56] Actually, divine immanence does not fare better when the borderline between uncreated and created life grows dimmer and dimmer (cf. Moltmann's "immanent transcendence" of life in open systems). If etymology were the key to meaning, "panentheism" would be acceptable (Acts 17:28); but, since the word was coined by Krause, it is used to soften resistance to pantheism, to decorate a milder or more timid form of pantheism.[57]

And yet I show you a more excellent way . . . From an altogether different quarter in the theological microcosm, from the "radical reformed" pole, comes a contribution to trinitarian theology that is worth pondering.

53. See the papers presented at the Third Edinburgh Conference in Christian Dogmatics, Nigel M. de S. Cameron, ed., *Power and Weakness of God: Impassibility and Orthodoxy* (Edinburgh: Rutherford House Books, 1990).

54. For more than mere samples, as offered here, refer to my *Christologie* (Vaux-sur-Seine: Fac-étude, 1986), 2 vols.

55. Jüngel, vol. 1, p. 118 (German: p. 102).

56. Jüngel, vol. 1, p. 145 n. 211 (German: p. 124).

57. The word "panentheism" was coined by Karl-Christian-Friedrich Krause (1781–1832). G. Ulrici comments: "eine oberflächliche Modifikation, die das Wesen und Prinzip der pantheistischen Weltanschauung gar nicht berührt." G. Ulrici, "Religionsphilosophie," in [Johann Jakob] Herzog, ed., *Real-Encyclopaedie für protestantische Theologie und Kirche,* vol. 12 (Gotha: Rudolf Besser, 1860), p. 717. Similarly, Karl Rahner, *Mission et grâce,* vol. 3, tr. into French by Charles Muller (Tours: Mame, 1965), p. 45 n. 3.

Cornelius Van Til, in his artless, almost brutal, yet acute and profound, manner, has stressed God's ontological Trinity as the condition of his independence and effective sovereignty.[58]

If God is caught in the perennial dipolarity of the One and the Many, as the One opposed to the Many, he cannot claim real independence, absolute primacy and ultimacy. He is defined by reference to another principle than himself, he is included together with the plural world in a broader totality — he is *correlative*. In order for God to be autarkic, self-sufficient, "self-contained" (Van Til likes the phrase), *noncorrelative*, he needs to be the foundation of both unity and diversity, holding them eternally within himself: so is he as the triune God.

This insight is not unparalleled. It is noteworthy that Pannenberg comes very close to it. In his defense of monotheism, he argues lucidly: "The doctrine of the Trinity is consequently monotheistic: it does not merely think God, in a platonic fashion, as the One opposed to the Many, and, thus, barely opposed to the world — in fact, such an opposition would grant the world, or at least matter, as God's partner, divine status and primordiality."[59] Van Til, however, shows that only the *ontological* Trinity, not derived from economy in the order of being, can avoid that fateful result. Expressly, Pannenberg uses the word "correlate" *(Korrelat)*, "eternal correlate of the deity of the Father," for one aspect pertaining to Jesus' *human* reality.[60] He cannot solve the contradiction between his sound concern to maintain the ontological Trinity ("concrete monotheism"), and the construction of *his* Trinity from the man Jesus. God's transcendence requires the prior Trinity, and the asymmetrical structure between Creator and creature.

Interestingly, the powerful Jewish thinker Emmanuel Lévinas also denounces "correlativity."[61] In his zeal for transcendence, Lévinas sets forth the major contemporary alternative to Heidegger, waging war against totality and ontology. One recalls Abraham Heschel's original opening, when

58. Since Van Til's own presentation is found in fragments scattered in his works or in early works of noneasy access, the best synthesis is that of Rousas J. Rushdoony, "The One and the Many Problem — the Contribution of Van Til," in E. R. Geehan, ed., *Jerusalem and Athens: Critical Discussions on the Theology and Apologetics of Cornelius Van Til* (Nutley, NJ: Presbyterian & Reformed, 1971), pp. 339-48.

59. Pannenberg, "Die Subjektivität," p. 39 n. 34.

60. Pannenberg, *Systematische Theologie*, p. 337: "Damit tritt an der menschlichen Wirklichkeit der Person Jesu ein Aspekt hervor, der als ewiges Korrelat der Gottheit des Vaters zur Person Jesu gehört."

61. Lévinas, p. 45: "Une transcendance absolue doit se produire comme inintégrable . . . d'une façon qui ne soit pas seulement correlative. . . . *La corrélation n'est pas une catégorie qui suffit à la transcendance*" (emphasis his).

he rejected the priority of being: he discerned in the classical privilege of ontology the pagan attempt to subsume both God and the world under the same encompassing notion; he proclaimed creation first, with its nonsymmetrical pattern.[62] Lévinas's dazzling critique develops Heschel's helpful insight; yet, with such deliberate excesses, such a strategy of hyperbolic thinking,[63] that he does not merely tread under foot every remnant of common sense, but departs from the teachings of Scripture. He brings his philosophy of *rupture* to the extreme of paradox. Ethical passion is absolutized, to the point of eclipsing God. The difficult, giddy idea of the infinite (the *'êin sôph* of Jewish mysticism) legitimates absolute discontinuities. In this, Lévinas shows himself to be the true heir of rabbinic subtlety and studied oddity, rather than the disciple of Moses and the Prophets.

Lévinas, however, remains a precious witness of the mutual exclusion of transcendence and correlativity. We must add, only, that the Trinity also grounds immanence: since God is Three, the world of plurality is no foreign territory to him; rather, he is at home among creatures that receive of him their being.

Servato discrimine personarum

Beyond the One and the Many consideration, can we discover still more precise connections between immanence, transcendence, and the actual figure of the Trinity? The classical adage *opera ad extra indivisa* would seem to rule this out, and, already, the truth of the divine essence existing only once. Transcendence and immanence characterize God's relationships *ad extra*, with the world; they are attributes, properties, or descriptions of his essence — the three Persons do not come into view.

Emil Brunner, however, reminds us that the maxim too often goes in a truncated form, and that it reads, if quoted in full: *opera ad extra indivisa SERVATO DISCRIMINE ET ORDINE PERSONARUM* — the distinction and order of the Persons being preserved.[64] Although there is one God, one divine essence, we should not separate the oneness from the threeness. Somehow, they belong to each other. The unity is *of* the Three, just as the

---

62. Abraham J. Heschel, *The Prophets II* (Harper Torchbooks; New York: Harper & Row, 1962, 1975 paperback), pp. 43-44. Lévinas does not mention Heschel.

63. Paul Ricoeur analyzes Lévinas's argument as a strategy of hyperbole in Ricoeur, *Soi-même comme un autre* (Paris: Seuil, 1990), pp. 387-93.

64. Emil Brunner, *Dogmatique I: la Doctrine chrétienne de Dieu*, tr. into French by Frédéric Jaccard (Geneva: Labor & Fides, 1964), p. 253.

Three are one God. If we sever the unbreakable bond, if we forget about the Trinity when thinking of the essence, we are missing the truth of the divine essence.

Divine unity rules out distinctions *in re*, that is, distinctions that would imply composition in God's being, with the possibility of real separation: *YHWH 'elohēnu YHWH 'ēḥad!* Yet, distinctions *ratione, cum fundamento in re*, distinctions we are invited to think, required not only by the debility of our subjective apprehension but by God's own reality, with objective validity, are to be maintained.[65] Hence the objectively valid distinction by St. Thomas Aquinas between the *principium quod* (the subject) and the *principium quo* (the essence), and the distinction between the various attributes.[66] Hence his strenuous, emphatic affirmation that the relations that constitute the three Persons are *real*. He calls them *relationes reales,* and he adds: *Relatio realiter existens in Deo habet esse essentiae divinae, idem ei existens,* "the relation, as it exists really in God, possesses the being of the divine essence, and it is identical with it."[67] Essence and Person (Relation) belong together.

The ontological ultimacy of the Trinity in God, implying, as it does, valid distinctions, makes it possible to see the reflection of the Three in the depiction of the divine essence, and, further in the *opera ad extra.* Conceivably, a trinitarian structure could be perceived, however dimly in the weakness of our eyes, in *every* attribute of God: the truth of every attribute is its possession by Father, Son, and Holy Spirit. But at this stage, trinitarian reflections are more easily recognized from the viewpoint of *appropriations.*

The doctrine of appropriations shines as a jewel of traditional theology. While it does not cease to confess, with no qualm, that attributes or works belong to all three Persons, it collects scriptural evidence of a special kinship, a privileged affinity, between *this* attribute and *that* Person. It does not mean an exclusive tie, but a significant correspondence: because attributes are truly diverse, and because essence is not indifferent to the threeness, being of-the-Three.

Transcendence, although we should ascribe it to Son and Spirit as well, is undoubtedly *appropriated to the Father.* The Father, ordinarily, answers

65. Jüngel, vol. 1, p. 167 n. 11 (German: p. 143), recalls the scholastic phrase *distinctio rationis ratiocinatae,* with the same import, objective validity, as contrasted with *distinctio rationis ratiocinantis.*

66. Malet, pp. 32-36, 99, 101.

67. St. Thomas Aquinas, *Summa theologiae* Iᵃ, Qu. 28, art. 1 and art. 2. Pannenberg argues that St. Thomas fails to establish his thesis (an "artificial," *gekünstelt,* thesis), and he relies on Duns Scotus. Pannenberg, *Systematische Theologie,* p. 321, with n. 124.

to the name *Theos* in the New Testament. As the first in the order of the Trinity, unbegotten, the one who sends and who is not sent, he exhibits most obviously the divine perfection of transcendence: *quo majus cogitari nequit*. Even if Jesus' words "The Father is greater than I" are set in the context of humiliation and incarnation, the Son's subordination, for all eternity according to 1 Corinthians 15:28, may not be erased from the biblical witness: it does not imply subordinationism; it does tell of trinitarian order. And, so, the divine *akhbar* is appropriated to the God and Father of all, who is above all . . . and also among all and in all — through the agency, we surmise, of his Son and of his Spirit (Eph. 4:6).

Immanence shows a similar *affinity with the Spirit*. The Spirit is the bearer of the divine presence: "Whither shall I go from thy Spirit, or whither shall I flee from thy presence?" (Ps. 139:7). The Spirit is pervading presence as the sustaining power of life (Ps. 104:29-30). He is so intimately united with created being that many passages remain ambiguous: do they speak of man's created breath or of God's own life-giving Breath? We may never identify the two, but how close they are! The Spirit is the indwelling presence: he is represented by the pillar of cloud, the symbol of God's residence in the midst of his people (Hag. 2:5 makes the identification); in the New Testament, the Spirit inhabits both the individual believer — whose body is the temple of the Holy Spirit — and the community, that building which grows "to be an habitation of God through the Spirit" (Eph. 2:21-22).

Can we spot a comparable connection with the Son, with the Wisdom whom God begat before the world began, with the image of the invisible God (this is sapiential language, echoing the Wisdom of Solomon 7:26 and referring to the preexistent *asarkos* condition), with the *Logos* who was in the beginning and through whom all things that have come into being were made? He is transcendent with the Father, Alpha and Omega, Lord of Lords. He fills everything as the Spirit does, being sent into the world. Yet the strongest appropriation of transcendence is to the Father, and of immanence to the Spirit.

The Son, Wisdom, image, *Logos*, distinctly guarantees the *vis-à-vis* structure within the Godhead. As the Father's alter ego, he stands face to face with the Father — *pros ton theon* (John 1:1). He is the object of the Father's love and the subject of responding love. We may even speak of covenant: older dogmaticians dared to call "covenant of redemption," concluded before the foundation of the world, the gift of the elect by the Father to the Son (John 6:37, 39; 10:29; 17:6; 18:9). As such, in deity itself, the Son has some correspondence with creation; creation is thus "in him." Hence the use of "image" both for him, eternally, and for that earthly creature who concentrates the meaning of creation: the human being. Hence the "fitness" (Heb. 1:10-11) of the Son's being made flesh, being made man. We would understand in this light his apocalyptic title: "The principle (*archē*) of God's creation" (Rev. 3:14).

The Son, the second Person in trinitarian order, prevents us from understanding transcendence and immanence in dialectical fashion; it is another configuration (to borrow Dr. Vanhoozer's word). And if the Son corresponds to creation, before creation, in God, then, it appears that a preface, *archē*, of transcendence and immanence obtains *within* trinitarian relationships. Transcendence and immanence in relation to the world do not change the divine identity when the world is created. They do not make God *correlative;* the glory of the ontological Trinity radiates in fullness, while it assures us that we, in the world, know God *himself* when he reveals himself: his revelation as the transcendent and immanent God is no alteration of his essence. We know him in grace and truth.

This is the logic, theo-logic, of John 1:18: the ontological Trinity is the ground of effective revelation — the only-begotten God who is in the bosom of the Father was free as such to explain God, in grace and truth.

· 8 ·

Karl Barth, the Trinity, and Pluralism

TREVOR HART

Introductory

The theme of our conference draws together into creative interaction two major concerns for the Christian theologian. Of one, the Trinity, Karl Barth had much to say, a fact more surprising in his generation than in ours, and one to which the current resurgence of interest in trinitarian theology owes no small amount. On the other topic (pluralism), however, Barth is, unsurprisingly, less forthcoming. For while the roots of contemporary pluralism lie buried deep in the philosophical soils of a century or more, and while its implications were already beginning to be worked out in the writings of theologians such as Troeltsch at the turn of the century, the pluralistic spirit that holds our age firmly in its grip has manifested itself clearly only in the years since Barth's death. It was not an issue in his day to the same degree that it is in ours.

This fact presents us with something of a problem. How to proceed? Are there sufficient materials to make an excursus into Barth's theology a worthwhile one with this particular combination of themes in mind? I believe that there are, although it will be clear from what has been said already that I shall not be attempting an exposition of Barth's own critical engagement with pluralism. Nor shall I be speculating as to what Barth might have said if he had survived to his one hundredth year and witnessed for himself the growing dominance of pluralistic views in the academy and other circles. What I hope to do instead is to approach his theology with the broad outlines of the contemporary discussion in view and to ask whether Barth himself may be construed as a pluralist of any sort. Does

124

the thrust of the overall scheme of his theology as it emerges in the *Church Dogmatics*[1] and elsewhere lend itself to a form of what might be called "soft" pluralism? Or is Barth a theologian who, in a stalwart defense of the universal truth of the gospel of Jesus Christ, altogether eschews pluralism in all its forms?

This, I hope to suggest, is not so easy a question to resolve as might at first seem to be the case. To some it may seem outrageous even to entertain the hypothesis that one whose name is so closely allied to such phrases as "the triumph of grace" and "a positivism of revelation" (neither of them Barth's own) could be thought guilty of pluralism of any kind. One who includes the views of many other Christians under the category of "heresy" and classifies human religion outside the Church as essentially a manifestation of "unbelief," it might reasonably be argued, can hardly be taken seriously as a candidate for classification among the pluralists! This observation (while it is crudely and unfairly couched here) carries a significant amount of weight, and such considerations even when qualified and more subtly and fairly presented certainly rule Barth out as a pluralist of a certain sort. But, as I shall suggest shortly, we may differentiate between different sorts, and there are elements within the overall superstructure of Barth's theology that point strongly to the compatibility of his theological project with a certain understanding of what a feasible epistemological pluralism might consist in. It is not for nothing that Lindbeck[2] points to suggestive parallels between his own so-called cultural-linguistic model of doctrine and Barth's approach to dogmatics. Just how far can these parallels be pushed before they topple?

Pluralism Agnostic and Committed

In order to pursue this discussion further I want at this point to borrow a careful and significant distinction drawn by Bishop Lesslie Newbigin.[3] The contemporary intellectual scene is often portrayed as if the decline of modernism and the ascent of postmodernist perspectives has left us with two basic options: on the one hand an optimistic objectivism of either an empiricist or rationalist variety; and on the other hand a pluralism that is

---

1. Karl Barth, *Church Dogmatics* (Edinburgh: T & T Clark).
2. George Lindbeck, *The Nature of Doctrine* (London: SPCK, 1984), p. 24.
3. See, e.g., Lesslie Newbigin, *Truth to Tell: The Gospel as Public Truth* (Grand Rapids: Eerdmans, 1991), pp. 56-57.

essentially relativistic and skeptical. We may either embrace the certainty afforded us by alleged universal truths of morality and reason, or by a hard-nosed concern with "facts," or else, disillusioned with these, throw in our lot with those whose only absolute commitment is to an uncompromising belief that such certainty is a will-o'-the-wisp, and that truth, if there is such a thing, lies utterly beyond our epistemic capacities. Certainty or despair; these, many commentators would seem to want us to believe, are the only options. It must be said at once that neither of them is particularly attractive for the Christian theologian, although across the theological spectrum they seem to have seduced roughly equal numbers. Part of what Barth saw in his day remains true in ours; namely, that very often theological "liberals" and "conservatives" are united in their basic methodologies and in the tools that they brandish as weapons with which to destroy one another's fortified positions. That which each despises in the other's point of view is often simply a distorted mirror image of their own basic presuppositions and procedures. While they appear to be utterly different, therefore, in truth they are twins, separated at birth and raised in wholly different environments, unable to identify precisely what it is about the other that so angers them when they meet face to face.

Part of what Lesslie Newbigin has been trying to do in his recent publications is to draw our attention away from the particular alternatives of objectivism and relativism and to point to a third way. His choice is to describe this way as a variant of pluralism, although the semantic associations of the word are immediately ruptured by its use in a quite distinct epistemic framework.

There is, Newbigin tells us, on the one hand "agnostic pluralism." This is pluralism of the sort with which we are quite familiar and with which we have been primarily concerned in this conference so far. It is the point of view that celebrates plurality and diversity for its own sake, viewing it as part of the richness of our human situation, and preferring it in every respect to any alleged or attempted uniformity of outlook or understanding. Emerging from the gradual realization that the eighteenth-century quest for a certain reliable and universally accessible basis for knowing has, over the course of two hundred years or more, failed time and time again to render its promised results, this pluralism arises from the despairing assumption that truth (if there be such) is unknowable to humans, and lies far beyond any of our several versions of it. This being so, it stands to reason that any and every claim to truth in anything more than a coherentist sense (i.e., something is true because it coheres with an overall view of things) must be denounced as a lapse into tribalism, an intolerance of the other for which, in our postmodern age, there can no longer be any excuse or any room. Above all, the attempt to convert, to change the mind of the other until he or she sees things differently, is palpable violence and can result only in the sort of partisan conflict that we have now left behind as the by-product of a darker age. Openness, tolerance, humility before the great mystery of life; these are the hallmarks of a truly pluralistic and liberal society. Hence necessity is seized and turned sagely into a virtue. We are, after all, all in the same epistemological boat, so we might as well own up to and make the best of our circumstances. No one has access to the way things really are. All our perspectives are physically, socially, historically, and culturally determined. No one way of seeing things can be deemed better or worse than another. The differences that divide us from one another must not be categorized in evaluative terms, since no criteria exist for making any such evaluation, or choosing any one point of view over another. We can compare our own way of thinking and seeing things only with that of others, never with the way things really are. The responsible mode of relation to others, therefore, is to occupy the context granted us by historical and social accident, and then to seek to supplement and enrich it by borrowing the insights of other traditions as and when we are able to access them. Thereby we may become more rounded and fulfilled human persons, better equipped in the quest for the great enigma of truth. The quest itself, however, must continue, for it is in principle and by definition endless.

Newbigin's second category is "committed pluralism." This, he suggests, is a stance that concurs in certain basic respects with agnostic pluralism but differs substantially at key junctures. Hence the committed pluralist too has learned from the failure of universalist objectivism, and concedes that there is no detached standpoint from which to view the world, but only a diverse series of perspectives, some of which are utterly incompatible with one another. Such quantities as rationality and morality, far from being the paracontextual bedrock of "what every intelligent human person knows to be true," are themselves inseparable from the warp and woof of historically and socially particular frameworks of meaning. What counts as a rationally or morally compelling case for one person, therefore, may be deemed irrelevant or wholly irrational/immoral by another. Such clashes of framework demonstrate the futility of simple appeals to reason in apologetic exercises and the verity of pluralism in its contention that the way we see things depends largely on where we happen to find ourselves. While, however, in rejecting objectivism, agnostic pluralism risks rapid collapse into its logical opposite of subjectivism and ultimate solipsism, the

TREVOR HART

committed pluralist remains what may be termed a critical realist. He remains, that is to say, committed to the view that pluralism is a feature of human knowing rather than of the way things are beyond human knowing, and optimistic in the capacity of humans to establish genuine and reliable epistemic contact with reality. Truth is there to be known, and may be known, if not absolutely or in any "objective" or universally compelling manner, then at least with sufficient certainty and in a mode that compels what Michael Polanyi refers to as knowledge-claims bearing "universal intent." Reality can be known by placing oneself in the places where it makes itself known, by viewing it from certain standpoints rather than others, by employing certain physical and conceptual tools rather than others, and so on. The knowledge obtained thereby is not of the absolutely certain variety craved by Descartes and those who followed in his wake, but is rather built on the precise foundations that he eschewed: namely, personal trust and faith. Polanyi presents this as the basic *modus operandi* of scientific knowing, notwithstanding the objectivist myths perpetrated and exalted even in our day concerning scientific procedure as a public enterprise.

The rub with all this, of course, is that it still breaches the code of tolerance as defined by modern liberal sympathies. To suggest that truth makes itself known or is in some (even partial) way knowable from one particular perspective with its assumptions and tools is thereby inevitably to claim for this perspective some superiority over others, and hence to assert their relative falsity. This, as I have suggested, is the one great unforgivable sin, if we could be certain that there is such a thing as sin, which, of course, we can't! But in fact, as Newbigin and those upon whose thought he draws at this point (notably Polanyi and Alasdair MacIntyre) suggest, the attitude that this committed stance fosters is not one of arrogance or dismissive intolerance, but precisely one of humility and openness. Since such truth-claims are nondemonstrable in the sense usually intended by that term, and since the knower knows only on the basis of a personal commitment to certain fundamental assumptions, she has no universally recognized or intellectually superior case with which to bludgeon those who do not stand where she does, or on the basis of which to call into question their intelligence or common sense. She, as one who believes that truth is indeed to be known in one way rather than another, but who must submit in her knowing to reality itself in its willingness to be known, can only enjoin those who see things radically differently to "come and stand where I am standing, view the world from this place and using these tools, and see whether what you find here doesn't make more sense." Thus if the mode of certainty is that of faith, then the mode of proclamation is that of witness.

128

(The resonances with the situation of the Christian believer, and the Christian theologian, are apparent even at this level.) There is a moral component to the committedness of committed pluralism. For the person who believes sincerely that reality grants itself to be known in one way and one place rather than in others, albeit not in any absolute or exhaustive or controllable manner, there is on the one hand an obligation to seek it there and not elsewhere (Martin Luther: "Here I stand; I can do no other . . ."), and on the other hand a charge to proclaim this "good news" that the despair of skepticism is not the only alternative to Descartes's project. Universal intent demands that we do so.

The thesis of the rest of this paper will be that it is possible to read Karl Barth, and his treatments of the doctrine of the Trinity and human religion in particular, as operating within the boundaries of a committed pluralism of this sort. Let us return, briefly, to the suggested parallel with Lindbeck in order to discern its limits.

Dogmatics as Grammar?

The Church, according to Barth, is constituted as the Church by its faithful hearing of the divine Word, the address of God himself, and its obedience in the task of handling this same Word and handing it on to others. In this way the central act of the Church is one in which, even in its essential humanness, it becomes the vehicle of divine self-giving to the world. But the Church is very much a human entity. And for this reason the question of its faithful acquittal of this responsibility must be faced. "When the church receives the Word," Barth writes, "the question has to arise: To what extent is the address that takes place in Christian preaching identical with the address that took place through the prophets and apostles. . . . To what extent is it the *Word of God?*"4 What is God's Word? What, that is to say, is God saying? And how is what is being said in the preaching of the Church related to this Word? It is with this question that Barth sees the dogmatician as primarily concerned. Dogmatics is the scientific or reflective self-examination of the Church with respect to its talk about God. It listens to what is said, and offers judgments. It acts in a normative, regulative, and corrective role, seeking to ensure (so far as is humanly possible) that what is said humanly from the pulpit coincides in some sense with what God has said and is saying to his Church. Thus "what

4. Karl Barth, *Göttingen Dogmatics*, vol. 1 (Grand Rapids: Eerdmans, 1991), p. 24.

dogmatics has to give" to the preacher "does not consist of contents but of guidelines, directions, insights, principles and limits for correct speech by human estimate."[5] Dogmatics, as it were, articulates the grammar of Christian speech about God, lays down the rules for speaking Christianly about him. It tells us "what will do and what will not do, what we may say and what we may not say if what we are to say is to be Christian preaching."[6] This essentially diagnostic and prophylactic role is necessary precisely because of the full humanity of the Church. "Dogmatics is required," says Barth, "because proclamation is a fallible work."[7] "In every age," he notes, "the church's preaching has been sick."[8]

This account of the essential activity of dogmatics certainly bears more than a passing resemblance to the "cultural-linguistic" model espoused by George Lindbeck in *The Nature of Doctrine*. Precisely the same regulative task is ascribed to the dogmatician. Thus, for Lindbeck, doctrines may be seen to be functioning "as communally authoritative rules of discourse, attitude and action."[9] They lay down rules of speech precisely similar to those to be found in the literal grammars of human speech. They regulate truth-claims by excluding some and allowing others, tolerating certain forms of speech as appropriate to and coherent with the reality and value system of the believing community (the "language"), and proscribing others as inappropriate and incoherent, as breaking the grammatical rules. Thus far this is utterly at one with Barth's understanding. There is, however, a fundamental difference between the two. For while in Lindbeck's account the criteria with which doctrine adjudges communal discourse are essentially empirical (i.e., "these are the rules" = "this is in fact the way the language has operated in the past") and the standards of truth and falsity purely coherentist (defined in terms of keeping the given rules), Barth will not rest content with this alone. The criteria with which dogmatics approaches its critical task are for him concerned not simply with the grammatical superstructure of a given language or system of beliefs, but with the reference of that same system beyond itself. They are not (to use Lindbeck's terms) simply intra-systemic, but radically extra-systemic. They concern a model of truth understood not in terms of coherence alone, but, in some sense at least, correspondence. In other words, the dogmatician

---

5. Barth, *Church Dogmatics*, 1/1 (Edinburgh: T & T Clark, 1975), p. 87.
6. Barth, *Göttingen Dogmatics*, 1, p. 18.
7. Barth, *Church Dogmatics*, 1/1, p. 82.
8. Barth, *Göttingen Dogmatics*, 11.III.16.
9. Lindbeck, p. 18.

does not simply ask, "How does this preaching measure up to traditional and communally acceptable ways of speaking about God?" but "How does this preaching measure up to the Word of God himself as he has given himself to be known?" There is, then, for Barth an objective criterion to be considered, a reality that gives itself to be known and to which he understands Christian preaching as referring. *Deus dixit.* God has spoken, and has been heard by the community of faith. That is the radical assumption of Christian proclamation, and therefore, indirectly, of Church dogmatics.

Revelation and the Givenness of Our Knowledge of God

Theology begins and ends with the self-revelation or self-proclamation of God in his living Word, incarnate in Jesus Christ, and attested in Scripture and the preaching of the Christian community. The familiar statement "God reveals Himself as the Lord"[10] is in a sense a recapitulation of the entirety of Christian dogmatics, referring us not only to the sole legitimate presupposition for theological activity, but also to the decisive shape to which that theologizing must conform if it is to be truly Christian. God has spoken, and that speaking alone furnishes a basis upon which the Church may in turn speak about God, and thereby grants theology its *raison d'etre*. God, Barth writes, "makes Himself present, known and significant to (men) as God. In the historical life of men He takes up a place, and a very specific place at that, and makes Himself the object of human contemplation, human experience, human thought and human speech."[11] This self-revealing, when it happens, does not allow itself to be understood as one option among many, or to be treated with indifference. It certainly cannot be set alongside human religion, or compared with the products of human religious endeavor as if it were something of the same sort. To view it thus is simply to misunderstand its true nature as revelation. "Revelation is understood only where we expect from it, and from it alone, the first and the last word about religion. . . . Revelation is God's sovereign action upon man or it is not revelation."[12]

God has spoken concerning himself. It is on this basis and this basis alone that the Church may speak about God. Every independent attempt by humans to know or speak about him is futile and doomed to failure. It

---

10. Barth, *Church Dogmatics*, 1/1, p. 295.
11. Barth, *Church Dogmatics*, 1/1, p. 315.
12. Barth, *Church Dogmatics*, 1/2 (Edinburgh: T & T Clark, 1956), p. 295.

131

is in this light that we must view human religion as an entity. However sincere it may or may not be, its fruit is, as Feuerbach rightly saw, essentially idolatrous, the projection of human needs and desires onto the clouds. Its failure is the failure to address itself to the proper place; the place where God has made himself known, and continues to make himself known. It is in this sense that Barth insists that human religion in and of itself is to be characterized as unbelief or faithlessness *(Unglaube)* and as such concluded under the condemnation of the cross. As we shall see, however, there is a subtle irony here that is too often missed by those who leap upon Barth's apparent intolerance of other religious possibilities. Revelation is indeed the abolition of religion. But the word *Aufhebung* also bears the ironic sense of lifting up or exaltation; and, since Barth concedes that Christianity too can be viewed humanly as a religion, what he seems to be suggesting here is that revelation indeed judges and puts to death human religious endeavor, but only in order that it may raise it up and set it upon a new and more glorious footing, just as in Christ our humanity in its entirety has been assumed, judged, crucified, and resurrected into a glorious new existence.

Barth's concern in emphasizing the place of revelation as the presupposition of theological activity is to insist that the logic of theological statements refers beyond human experience to a reality that provokes or creates that experience. The nineteenth century, with its various attempts to root and validate theological language in some aspect or other of human experience, had simply indulged Feuerbach's damning reduction of theological statements to theological language. Theology is not concerned to express or articulate the contents of experience, but rather to respond obediently to the form of God's own self-giving and self-revealing initiative, an initiative that is already couched in verbal, cognitive, and fleshly form: the humanity of Jesus Christ, the text of Scripture, and the preaching of the Church.

In all this there would seem to be little room for pluralism. In the event of revelation the truth of God stands over against us unconditionally. It will allow of no compromise, no bargaining, no partial or half-hearted response. What it demands of us and itself creates in us is obedience: an obedient hearing and speaking on the part of the Church. And what this hearing and speaking in fact has to report is, as we shall see, triune in structure. God is made known to us as Father, Son, and Holy Spirit. Henceforth, Barth insists, this trinitarian understanding must be heard whenever the term "God" is used in the Church. It must be placed at the head of all dogmatic endeavor as a determinative hermeneutical principle.[13] In answer

13. See Barth, *Church Dogmatics*, 1/1, p. 300.

to the all-determinative question "Who is the God in Whom we believe?" the Church must not fail to give this answer and this alone. To entertain belief in any other god, or to allow the term "God" to be defined differently for the sake of some apologetic argument or in pursuit of some common denominator of shared understanding, is simply to capitulate once again to the very idolatry from which revelation seeks to deliver us. Thus the doctrine of the Trinity, or rather the Church's proclamation of the triune God who has made himself known in revelation, cannot be set alongside other alternative models or ways of understanding as "one view among many," or one route to God among many. God has spoken and has been heard. That this is so rules out either agnosticism or the categorical substitutability of religious constructs as valid options for the Church. It can do only what it is called to do; namely, to bear witness to the truth that it knows.

Revelation as a Closed Circle of Knowing

And yet, Barth is in no way optimistic concerning the impact of such witness upon the world at large, at least in the short term. For this full-blooded affirmation of the possibility and actuality of true knowledge of God, while it certainly flies in the face of agnostic pluralism, does not embrace any form of universalistic objectivism as its alternative. (It should be noted that the term "objectivism" here is used in the sense defined earlier in this paper, rather than in the specific sense given to it by George Hunsinger in his book *How to Read Karl Barth*.)[14] There is no succumbing to the temptation to appeal to the self-evidently rational or moral, nor to some objectively given and self-authenticating universal revelation that the Church may control and use at will.

For Barth revelation is to be understood not as some abstract historical quantity, nor as a body of knowledge or data to which all humans in principle have equal access. The Church may and must direct people to the human Jesus, to the text of Scripture, and to its own preaching, for these are the forms that the Word of God takes in the sphere of the human. But they are not to be confused with revelation itself, which is the event *(Ereignis)* in which these various creaturely realities become pregnant with revelatory power for us in such a way that God speaks and is heard by particular

14. George Hunsinger, *How to Read Karl Barth* (London: Oxford University Press, 1991).

people. The human and the divine aspects of God's Word are *inseparabiliter* in this event; but they are equally *inconfuser*. God remains free and mysterious even in the midst of his self-limiting in revelation. He gives himself to be known, but not in such a way that he may be laid hold of or treated as an "object." Revelation takes human form in history, but it is not confinable within these human forms. Not all who met Jesus found themselves encountered by him as the Son of God. Not all who open the Bible discover in its words the words of eternal life. Not all who sit under the preaching of the gospel hear the gospel preached. Revelation is not historical in this sense.

The presupposition that lies behind Barth's view of revelation as an event in which human realities become the Word of God is that of the radical unknowability of God. "We have to admit," Barth writes, "that we cannot hear, feel, touch or either inwardly or outwardly perceive the one who reveals himself, not because he is invisible or pure spirit, but because he is God, because he is wholly himself, 'I am who I am,' the subject that escapes our grasp, our attempt to make him an object."[15] Again, "God does not belong to the world. Therefore He does not belong to the series of objects for which we have categories and words by means of which we draw the attention of others to them, and bring them into relation with Him. Of God it is impossible to speak, because He is neither a natural nor a spiritual object."[16] This, of course, would be the end of the story and the ultimate endorsement of the agnostic pluralist point of view were it not for one other thing: the fact that this same God has made himself known, has "objectified" himself that we might lay hold of him. But he has done so and does so in such a way that he becomes that which is not God, enters the realm of the creaturely, lays himself before us in a form that we are capable of receiving. But the form, as that which is not God, is not to be confused with revelation as such. It makes revelation possible. It furnishes the conditions under which it may take place. The creaturely form itself, however (whether we think of the human Jesus, the text of Scripture, or the words of Christian preachers), serves as much to conceal the divine reality as to reveal it. In order for revelation to happen (and, as *Ereignis*, "happen" is precisely what it does) there must be in, with, and under this human form a specific self-giving of God to particular persons, an unveiling of himself, a granting of eyes to see and ears to hear.

It is in his reflection upon the event of revelation that Barth discerns

15. Barth, *Göttingen Dogmatics*, 1, p. 9.
16. Barth, *Church Dogmatics*, 1/2, p. 750.

the logic of the doctrine of the Trinity. God exists as the unknowable and unspeakable Lord. Yet this same God objectifies himself as other, in such a way that he is over against himself as revelation over against revealer. But, if human persons are to receive this revelation, then, since they possess no natural aptitude to do so, it is necessary for this self-objectification to be accompanied by another, this time one in which God indwells us directly and creates in us the subjective conditions for receiving the Word that he speaks; namely, the Holy Spirit, who creates faith and obedience. As this event happens, the veil is lifted and we perceive the Word of God in the flesh of Jesus, the words of Scripture, and preaching. But even once this has happened there is no sense in which we are able to lay hold of these creaturely objects and wring from them God's Word. Precisely because revelation is an event, a relationship that "straddles objectivity and subjectivity"[17] and in which we are effectively drawn into the triune life of God, knowing the Father through the Son in that koinonia which is created by the Spirit, it must be new every morning, or else it has petrified and is not revelation at all but merely the empty form from which life has passed. Revelation as such cannot be grasped, held on to, or controlled by the human knower. We know only as we are in turn known by a God who draws us into relationship with himself. This same God it is who determines to whom he will reveal himself.

What all this mounts to, then, is a claim by Barth that the truth of God is known only from within what he describes as "a self-enclosed circle,"[18] namely, the triune circle of God's self-knowing, into which humans are drawn in the event of revelation. This revelation, therefore, is not universally known or knowable, and humans have no natural aptitude for it. It is an act of sovereign grace on the part of God himself when anyone finds himself drawn into it. Christian theology, if it is done at all, is done only within this same circle in obedient response to the self-giving of God. Thus the truth that it refers us to, the arguments that it deploys, the language that it chooses are all radically contextual, and the theologian certainly cannot look forward to any straightforward endorsement or recognition of them by the intellectual community at large. Only for those who indwell the same framework of meaning, who view the world with the same eyes, will what is said here make any real sense. For Barth this in no way compromises the universal intent of theological statements. It simply means

---

17. Christina Baxter, "The Nature and Place of Scripture in the Church Dogmatics," in J. Thompson, ed., *Theology beyond Christendom* (Allison Park, PA: Pickwick, 1986), p. 35.
18. See, e.g., Barth, *Church Dogmatics*, 1/2, p. 280.

that they are precisely Church statements, statements of a faith shared by a community of knowing, a community that is both synchronic and diachronic in nature, but that is in many ways set over against the world as a scandal. Here, then, the doctrines of election and of the Holy Spirit serve to underwrite something very close to a committed pluralism of the sort that Newbigin describes. Those who are drawn into this circle, who are granted "eyes to see," are thereby given to see what cannot otherwise, from other perspectives, be seen. Faith, as a moral relation to God in Jesus Christ, a participation in the very inner life of God, is thus precisely a relation that grants "conviction of things not seen." From this there follow some clear implications for the way in which the Church may handle the truth-claims that it is compelled to make over against those who indwell or espouse other worlds of meaning and discourse.

Apologetics and *Vestigia trinitatis*

Brief mention must therefore be made of that aspect of Barth's thought with which most students of theology will be familiar at least in broad terms; namely, his resolute opposition to all forms of natural theology.

Barth defines natural theology as follows: "every . . . formulation of a system which claims to be theological, i.e. to interpret divine revelation, whose *subject*, however, differs fundamentally from the revelation in Jesus Christ and whose *method* therefore differs equally from the exposition of Holy Scripture."[19] Barth's rejection of all such apologetic enterprises rests precisely on a conviction that the logic of the gospel is not universally accessible, but can be grasped only in the moral venture of faith as people indwell the Christian gospel itself as their primary world of meaning. Apologetics, in most of its traditional forms at least, begins with the opposite assumption, that some universal canon or index of rationality exists, to which the gospel may be brought for justification. This may be couched in terms of a "general revelation" rather than suggesting any essentially autonomous Promethean storming of the heavens by human reason, but the key point for Barth is that it is posited as prior to and independent of the specific self-giving of God in Jesus Christ and the Holy Spirit. There is, he is adamant, no such *preparatio evangelica* to which the truths of Christian faith may be brought for approval and recognition, or to which apologetic

19. Karl Barth, *Natural Theology*, tr. Peter Fraenkel (London: The Centenary Press, 1946), pp. 74-75.

appeal may be made, therefore, in the task of proclaiming Christ to those who do not know him.

The truth of the gospel is self-authenticating and self-involving for those to whom it manifests itself. They cannot deny it once they have encountered it, but can only point others to it in the hope that they too may see it. To see it, to hear and obey it, is to enter into the community of faith in which life is lived in accordance with the gospel. But the harsh fact of the matter is that to those who do not yet see it, to whom it has not revealed itself, it remains utterly hidden. There can be no partial knowing, no preparing of the ground or preparing the Way of the Lord here. The gospel cannot legitimately be brought to some other, more ultimate, human court of appeal in an attempt to secure for it a hearing. In fact, it seems that the opposite is true, that, far from commending itself to some inherent sense of truth and goodness in humans, the gospel is received as a scandal, a word that contradicts accepted norms and mores. What we must be ever mindful of, however, Barth insists, is the fact that we are not dealing here with a gospel that is scandalous to some supposed "human reason," since such is an abstract fiction. Rather we are dealing with a clash between the faith commitments of the Christian community and those of other communities as they find articulation in contextually normative canons of rationality and credibility. It is unbelief to which the gospel is a scandal; a commitment to other truths, other gospels, other gods. Once this is seen, then the reckless folly (perhaps blasphemy is not too strong a word?) of seeking to afford the gospel warrant by appealing to prior canons of acceptability is manifest. It is to seek to justify faith on the basis of terms laid down by sinful unbelief, to bring Yahweh to Baal for his blessing.

It is in this light that what Barth has to say about the so-called *vestigia trinitatis* makes sense. The doctrine of the Trinity, he affirms, is given to the Church in both the form and the content of the divine Word that is spoken in its midst and that it is in turn commanded to speak. In terms of an understanding of the very word "God," which the Church shares with other religious traditions (a fact about which the Church has cause to be somewhat uneasy and which must lead it to be careful in its use of the word), it is this doctrine that "basically distinguishes the Christian doctrine of God as Christian"[20] and that must therefore be set forth clearly at the outset of all Christian speech about God in order both to avoid any possible confusion as to the meaning of "God" and to provide unshamed testimony to this truth by which the Church lives. At this point, therefore, Barth sets

20. Barth, *Church Dogmatics,* 1/1, p. 301.

his face against the pluralist theologies of religion of the present day, in which such distinctive awkwardnesses for interfaith dialogue as the Trinity, the incarnation, and the atonement are conveniently classified in such a way that they can be set aside as mere matters of language, and attention directed rather to what is considered to be really important, namely some alleged predoctrinal ethical or experiential common ground between Christianity and other religious traditions. There can be little doubt that Barth would view such procedures as lacking in integrity and as rendering genuine dialogue (i.e., an informed meeting of different viewpoints in which participants both hear and respect difference as difference, rather than seek to obliterate it or swallow it up into some amorphous experiential uniformity) impossible. An interesting account of just what such dialogue between genuinely different traditions and worlds of meaning might look like is given by Alasdair MacIntyre in his *Whose Justice? Which Rationality?* [21] His account is one that my reading of Barth encourages me to think the latter might well have found congenial.

To return, however, to the matter of the *vestigia trinitatis:* notwithstanding the origin of trinitarian understanding in the very mode and manner of God's self-revealing activity, the history of Christian theology is littered with attempts to commend this particular doctrine on grounds other than this revelation itself, grounds that might render it more believable or palatable to the non-Christian, or that might at least be adduced as a confirmation of or support for what God in his revelatory act shows us of himself. Thus, appeals have been made to aspects of God's creature to show that the notion of triunity, far from being an outrage to common sense, or an enigma, finds echoes, parallels, and virtual foretellings in human psychology, in the formal properties of water and other elements, in the energy produced by the sun, and so forth. Popular apologetics as well as its theological counterpart is full of such. And, of course, there are the inevitable attempts to find hints toward or even alternate versions of the doctrine of the Trinity in other religions, whether pre-Christian or non-Christian. And somehow all this is meant to make the doctrine of the Trinity itself more worthy of our acceptance, and more commendable to others.

Barth's rejection of such apologetic devices does not begin with an outright denial that there may indeed be facets of our human experience that, viewed from a certain perspective, seem to bear some sort of crude similarity to the Church's confession of God who is one in three and three

---

21. Alasdair MacIntyre, *Whose Justice? Which Rationality?* (Notre Dame: University of Notre Dame Press, 1989), see esp. ch. 19.

in one. Rather, his concern is one of method, and concerns the inevitable suggestion that the doctrine of the Trinity itself may have some other basis than that given it in God's self-revealing manifestation in his Son, and might actually either require or receive warrant from some other set of considerations or criteria than those provided by the gospel itself. This, he is convinced, is to misunderstand the situation. On the one hand, the one who has been encountered by the triune God does not need such bolstering or confirming of the truth of God's triunity. It is given in the very structure of the gospel, and of the way, therefore, in which she makes sense of or experiences the world. On the other hand, the person who has not had any such encounter will hardly be brought closer to it (since it rests upon God's sovereign freedom and grace alone) by having such fascinating parallels placed before him, and may, indeed, lacking the eyes through which such analogies may be viewed in the light of the analogate, be led into all sorts of misunderstanding and error in his thinking about this matter. If there are *vestigia*, then, for Barth, they could only be recognized by faith from within the framework of understanding and believing determined by the gospel. To direct those who stand elsewhere to them in the search for faith, therefore, is like sending someone into hazardous terrain on a quest to find the map and compass that would guide them and enable them to navigate it safely. If they ever arrive at the intended destination, it will be in spite of, and not because of, the strategy.

Christianity the One True Religion

Barth has no qualms about referring to Christianity as the only "true" religion; but his attitude toward religious alternatives, far from being dismissive or arrogant, is one characterized by respect and humility. It is not, however, a humility that would seek to endorse or commend the existence of such alternatives and what they do as good in themselves, but rather that of a sinner among sinners, who feels that his own glass home is rather too fragile for him to be throwing any stones.

Christianity itself, Barth reminds us, is in its human aspect precisely a religion. Like all other religions, it is in this respect not some prior receptivity for God or some aptitude to receive him, but precisely a self-assertiveness over against God, an attempt to lay down the terms on which it will deal with him. It is characterized by an a priori grasping after truth rather than a willingness to have truth granted to it freely and unconditionally. "Because it is a grasping, religion is the contradiction of revelation, the concentrated expression of human unbelief, i.e. an attitude and activity which is directly opposed to faith. It is a feeble but defiant, an arrogant but hopeless, attempt to create something which man could do, but now cannot do, or can do only because and if God himself creates it for him: the knowledge of the truth, the knowledge of God."[22] That this truth is known, that faith is created among humans, is therefore a matter of pure grace, and Christianity *as a religion* is no more capable of it than any other religious manifestation. Indeed, that the Church itself is quite capable of unbelief, of a religiosity that distances God rather than draws nearer to him, is clear enough from its history and from any phenomenological survey of its practices. Thus the abolition of religion by revelation applies just as surely to Christianity as to every other religious tradition. Time and time again God makes himself known to us in ways that cut through and call into judgment the conceptual idols with which we so quickly replace him when left to ourselves.

The outcome of all this, however, is not the despairing conclusion that all religious traditions are equally false (and therefore equally true). Barth is quick to confirm that in Christianity, notwithstanding its essential and sinful humanity, we may speak of the existence of a true religion; but only in precisely the same sense that we speak of a justified sinner.[23] In God's gracious election the Church becomes the place, the community, where God makes himself known in spite of its religiosity. This gracious choice rests not upon any intrinsic or inherent religious or ethical qualities that the Church possesses, but rather upon the sovereign grace of God alone. "If we look at the Christian religion in itself and as such," Barth writes, "we can only say that apart from the clear testimony of the fact of God some other religion might equally well be the right and true one. But once the fact of God is there and its judgment passed, we cannot look at the Christian religion in itself and as such."[24] We can only view it as it appears to the eyes of faith, namely as "the sacramental area created by the Holy Spirit, in which the God whose Word became flesh continues to speak through the sign of His revelation."[25] Thus the *Aufhebung der Religion* is like the cross in John's Gospel, paradoxically both the crucifixion and the "lifting up" of humanity.

One more thing must be said. If it is election and forgiveness that bestow upon the church the status of being the place where the truth about

22. Barth, *Church Dogmatics*, 1/2, pp. 302-3.
23. Barth, *Church Dogmatics*, 1/2, p. 326.
24. Barth, *Church Dogmatics*, 1/2, p. 354.
25. Barth, *Church Dogmatics*, 1/2, p. 359.

God is made known, they equally bestow upon it a greater degree of responsibility than pertains to other communities, other traditions. If the sin of religion is committed in the church, then it is committed "with a high hand" and is at once more needful of the very grace that establishes and nourishes it.[26] Human religion, even in its finest manifestations, constitutes idolatry and self-righteousness. But it only appears as such from within the place where the one true God makes himself known. "The man to whom the truth has really come will concede that he was not at all ready and resolved to let it speak to him."[27] Those who do not stand here, who have not stood here, find themselves possessed of greater excuse, therefore, than those who have and do stand here, and still perpetuate the sin of idolatry and unbelief. It is in this sense that Barth finds himself forced to adopt a tolerant and respectful attitude toward those whose standpoint does not afford them a view of the truth that has drawn him into its sphere of manifestation and influence. If his conviction of this truth and his refusal to compromise it lead Barth to be arrogant and harsh in his attitude, then it is not toward the occupants of other frameworks, but precisely toward those who see and live life out of the same truth as himself, but who take their relationship to it for granted and thereby presume upon grace.

By Way of Conclusion

We conclude, then, by reminding ourselves that for Barth the doctrine of the Trinity (and the Christian gospel of which it may be taken as a representative in this respect) constitutes a truth-claim with aspirations to correspondence, rather than being of a merely coherentist variety. This does not suppose any crude or naive linguistic understanding in Barth (such as that caricatured by Lindbeck under the label of "cognitive-propositional"), but rather indicates that *in some sense* the mode of theological statements is one in which they refer beyond themselves and beyond the particular framework of the belief structure of the Christian community (the "language" in Lindbeck's sense) to the reality of God himself.[28] They can do this only because God himself has taken human language and drawn it into

26. Barth, *Church Dogmatics*, 1/2, p. 337.
27. Barth, *Church Dogmatics*, 1/2, p. 302.
28. For a helpful discussion of Barth's understanding of theological language in this respect, see G. Hunsinger, "Beyond Literalism and Expressivism: Karl Barth's Hermeneutical Realism," *Modern Theology* 3, no. 3 (1987): 209-10.

the service of his self-revealing and redemptive gospel. Nonetheless, this reference functions and this language makes sense only within the context of this particular faith community as the place where God has made and makes himself known. To those who indwell other frameworks, who speak other languages, it remains foreign, an enigma, or even a scandal to be mocked. This does not mean that the doctrine of the Trinity is true only for those who belong here, but rather that "here" is the only place where its truth may be grasped and truly articulated. Theological statements are therefore truth-claims bearing universal intent, although they can claim no universal demonstrability, but rest on a series of ultimate faith commitments that, like all others, remain vulnerable to rejection and mockery.

In all these respects, I suggest, Barth's understanding of the status of doctrinal statements fits neatly together with what Newbigin has described as a "committed pluralist" epistemology. Neither a despairing agnosticism nor a confident objectivism (and the imperialistic apologetics that is its logical corollary) is acceptable to Barth. The gospel is "public truth" in Newbigin's sense, but not truth that can be forced down the throats of unbelievers with the strong arm of rationally compelling argument. On the other hand, Barth has no time whatever for the suggestion that at the end of the day we should simply allow unbelief to go unchallenged or content in its own alternative religious or irreligious outlook. God has revealed himself, and commands us to make his name known among the nations. The gospel is precisely for those who do not yet know its redeeming power, and the charge to the Church is to proclaim it boldly. It has "universal intent."

The mode of knowing in this "pluralistic" circumstance is that which the Church has always owned — namely, faith with all its attendant risks; and the mode of proclamation that which, when it has been faithful to its calling, the Church has adopted — namely, witness. That Barth's theology is so evidently structured around an acceptance of this fact makes it a potentially fruitful working example of the sort of third way between objectivism and relativistic pluralism to which secular philosophers are increasingly pointing as the epistemic reality of every human rational undertaking. A recognition of this claim, and an attempt to face up to its implications in other spheres of knowing, would seem to provide the only satisfactory way out of the postmodern malaise.

• 9 •

Karl Rahner, the Trinity, and Religious Pluralism

GARY BADCOCK

Karl Rahner's dictum that "the 'economic' Trinity is the 'immanent' Trinity, and the 'immanent' Trinity is the 'economic' Trinity,"[1] is well known and almost universally cited with approval in recent trinitarian theology. What is not so well known, however, is the content of Rahner's own trinitarianism, or even what he himself meant by his famous dictum when it was first formulated. The purpose of this paper is to explore and critique Rahner's trinitarian position with reference to his wider theology, and to pose the question of its relevance to the problem of interreligious dialogue.

Prescinding from all the more obvious potential or actual variations of content in different versions of the doctrine of the Trinity, it might be said that there are, from a more formal point of view, only two possible approaches to the doctrine. On the one hand, the Trinity can be seen *sub specie aeternitatis,* in terms of its intrinsic being first of all, and, following from this, in terms of its outreach to the world; here we have the bulk of the development of the doctrine in Christian theology, according to which the trinitarian structure of Christian dogmatics is determined by the being of God and the divinely initiated events of creation, incarnation, and Pentecost. In this way, the dogmatic enterprise is ordered fundamentally in terms of the God who is triune, and who in his triune identity creates, reconciles, and sanctifies. On the other hand, it is possible to approach the doctrine

---

1. Karl Rahner, *The Trinity,* tr. Joseph Donceel (London: Burns and Oates, 1970), p. 22, emphasis deleted.

143

of the Trinity from the point of view of the human being who is in search of God, "from below," *sub specie temporis,* as it were, rather than "from above." On this view, the doctrine of the Trinity is developed as the principle that orders the spiritual life; rather than being concerned with the divine approach to us, in other words, we are here concerned with our approach to God. While the latter must at some stage be conceived as a function of the former in any theology that, like Rahner's, seeks to sustain the priority of grace, it is possible for a trinitarian theology to be primarily a theology of the spiritual life rather than of the divine life — to be concerned basically, in short, with our approach to God rather than with God's approach to us.

Rahner's entire theological enterprise, and his trinitarian position within it, must be conceived as an instance of such a theological approach "from below." An adequate appreciation of his trinitarianism, therefore, is predicated upon an awareness that his theology of the Trinity is approached from the standpoint of the theology of the spiritual life. For this reason, theological anthropology lies at the heart of Rahner's theology as a whole, for it is in our theological anthropology that we conceive ourselves as human precisely and supremely in relation to God. Two correlative terms belong together in Rahner's theology at this point, the first, the self-communication of God, and the second, the self-transcendence of human beings. The divine self-communication to human beings is such that God himself becomes a constitutive principle of human being as such; human self-transcendence is such that there is a development from below to what is higher, from matter to spirit, from fact to truth and value, and from truth and value to absolute truth and absolute value. The history of human self-transcendence is also the history of the self-communication of God to humanity. At the pinnacle of this history, where both the divine self-communication and human self-transcendence reach their definitive expression, stands the Christ-event. But the inner mystery of even the Christ-event is also the innermost mystery of all human existence *as such,* for human being is, as Rahner puts it, the event of God's "free," "unmerited," and "absolute" self-communication.[2]

In short, Rahner's claim is that all human being as such is graced by the presence of God, and that it is precisely the closeness, the immediacy of God to us that is the source of all that is distinctively human in human life. On the other hand, Rahner's claim is that this closeness of God is also, and at the same time and in the same movement, the goal of human life, or something that has yet to be finally realized in the vision of God, which, according to Catholic

2. Karl Rahner, *Foundations of Christian Faith,* tr. W. V. Dych (London: Darton, Longman and Todd, 1978), pp. 116ff.

tradition, will constitute our eternal bliss. Rahner's theology is radical at this point for the simple reason that this immediacy of God, which he defines as the communication of the Holy Spirit or the gift of grace, is neither the preserve of the Christian nor exclusive to the religious life. It is not given in the first instance in conjunction with the gift of faith; rather, it is a deposit given to each and every human being, and it is, in the final analysis, that which is most true about them, that which makes them truly human, that which, at the summit of human potentiality, makes them capable of knowing and loving, and finally of knowing and loving God.

From this insight stems Rahner's celebrated doctrine of the "anonymous Christian," according to which each human being, presumably from the earliest humanoid capable of spiritual development in evolutionary prehistory, to each and every sinner or saint in the contemporary world, to the members of the non-Christian religions and the members of no religion, are recipients of the grace of God and therefore, implicitly or explicitly, members of the Christian Church.[3] There is thus a universal orientation in Rahner's theological anthropology, a certain generosity of scope, which he defends on the basis of his theology of grace. On the other hand, because Rahner is quite clear that the gift of grace can be resisted to varying degrees, just as it can be accepted to varying degrees, this universal orientation appears to stop somewhat short of universalism in the usual sense.[4] Nevertheless, the largesse of the grace of God in Rahner's theology is plain to see.

Human life, therefore, is for Rahner spiritual life and life capable of knowing and loving God because of the fact and to the extent that there is at the center of all human being a participation in God's being, founded on the divine self-communication. What is communicated, as Rahner puts it, is not information about God, or some nondivine, creaturely reality that mediates grace, but rather grace as the gift of God himself: "God in his own proper reality makes himself the innermost constitutive element of man."[5] Although this self-communication is often obscure to human experience — although,

---

3. Karl Rahner, "Anonymous Christians," in Rahner, *Theological Investigations*, vol. 6, tr. K. H. and B. Kruger (London: Darton, Longman and Todd, 1969), pp. 390-98; and Rahner, "Anonymous Christianity and the Missionary Task of the Church," in Rahner, *Theological Investigations*, vol. 12, tr. David Bourke (London: Darton, Longman and Todd, 1974), pp. 161-78.

4. Rahner argues, however, in "The Christian Understanding of Redemption," *Theological Investigations*, vol. 21, tr. H. M. Riley (London: Darton, Longman and Todd, 1988), p. 250, that ultimately the question whether all can finally be saved must be left to God, and therefore that it cannot be answered in theology.

5. Rahner, "The Christian Understanding of Redemption," p. 116.

for example, God seems at times to be remote and at times to be nowhere —
it also evidences itself a thousand times along life's way in the orientation of
human being as such to God. In itself, the immediacy of God is hidden away
in our unthematic subjectivity, but this closeness of God as the ground and
goal of human existence as spiritual, self-transcending reality emerges naturally and spontaneously through human experience. The task of Christian
theology must therefore be, at least in part, to provide a description of
ourselves, a phenomenology of the Spirit, that will bring what is so close to
us and thus so often unthematic to light.[6] Thus Rahner himself in his many
pastoral activities commonly attempted to bring those whom he counseled
to recognize that God was already with them, and that the root and goal of all
human existence is finally found in the simple acceptance of the primordial
grace of his presence.[7] Although supremely that grace comes to expression in
Christ, for Rahner, to restrict the grace of God to that Christological focus or
to those who believe in Christ would be to do the grace of God, and indeed
Christ himself, along with humanity as a whole, an untold injustice.

Thus the experience of God — whether in the thousand little moments of spiritual insight that constitute the best in human existence or in
the full-blown consciousness of God's saving will and work in the context
of an explicit (Catholic) Christian faith — constitutes the theological center
of Rahner's theology. In an extraordinarily revealing passage written near
the end of his life, which sums up much of his theological enterprise, Rahner
states:

> I have experienced God directly. I have experienced God, the nameless
> and unfathomable one, the one who is silent and yet near, in the trinity
> of his approach to me. I have really encountered God, the true and living
> one, the one for whom this name that quenches all names is fitting. God
> himself. I have experienced God himself, not human words about him.
> This experience is not barred to anyone. I want to communicate it to
> others as well as I can.[8]

As this passage suggests, it is fundamental to Rahner's thought that
this experience of God, and the self-communication of God on which it
rests, is trinitarian in structure. In the dense and often cryptic language of

6. Rahner, "The Christian Understanding of Redemption," p. 129.
7. See, e.g., Herbert Vorgrimler, *Understanding Karl Rahner*, tr. John Bowden (London:
SCM Press, 1986), pp. 1-44.
8. Karl Rahner, *Schriften zur Theologie*, vol. 15, pp. 374-75, as cited by Vorgrimler,
p. 11.

one of Rahner's best-known works, *The Trinity,* this structure in its economic aspect is defined in terms of truth and love as "the fundamental modalities of the divine self-communication."[9] Rahner here refers the modality of truth to what happened in history in Jesus Christ, and the modality of love to what happens in our present history as this truth is opened up toward the future in concrete existence, but what this might mean is left unexplained and unexplored. Elsewhere, however, it is possible to see in Rahner's theology a more detailed development of the themes of the self-communication of God and the experience of God as explicitly trinitarian in structure.

I shall argue in what follows that Rahner's theology as a whole is fundamentally a theology of the Holy Spirit, but this does not mean that he is without a Christology, or that he is without a theology of all that the term "Christology" classically implies: the doctrines of the eternal *Logos,* the incarnation, the hypostatic union, the *communicatio idiomatum,* and so on. Even more, it does not mean that Christology is incidental in his overall theology; indeed, Rahner goes so far as to state unequivocally that "the redemption of the human race means redemption through Jesus Christ."[10] On the other hand, Rahner consistently defines grace, which *is* the self-communication of God to you and me, in pneumatological rather than in Christological terms. Furthermore, Rahner positively rejects the idea that Christ lives, dies, and rises from death as our vicarious representative, in whom we find and experience the grace of God.[11] Indeed, instead of viewing the Christ-event as the unique and, because of its divine subject, the universal soteriological reality into which all human being must be incorporated through faith and the sacraments, according to the received wisdom, Rahner explicitly treats the incarnation and the content of Christology as continuous in its basis and meaning with the general self-communication of God to all human being as such.[12] Given the pneumatological content of the latter, one of Rahner's own collaborators has gone so far as to suggest that to be self-consistent, Rahner's Christology requires an explicitly pneumato-

9. Rahner, *The Trinity,* pp. 98-99.

10. Rahner, "The Christian Understanding of Redemption," p. 247.

11. Karl Rahner, "Reconciliation and Vicarious Representation," in *Theological Investigations,* vol. 21, pp. 255-69.

12. Karl Rahner, "Current Problems in Christology," in Rahner, *Theological Investigations,* vol. 1, 2nd ed., tr. Cornelius Ernst (London: Darton, Longman and Todd, 1965), pp. 149-200; and Rahner, "On the Theology of the Incarnation," in Rahner, *Theological Investigations,* vol. 4, tr. Kevin Smyth (London: Darton, Longman and Todd, 1966), pp. 105-20.

logical development[13] — although it must be said that this is something entirely missing in Rahner's own exposition of the Christological dogmas, where the human nature of Christ is related to the *Logos* rather than to *pneuma*.

The decisiveness of Christology, or, better, of Jesus Christ, in Rahner's theology is to be understood as deriving from the concreteness of the Christ-event in history. In Christ, God's forgiving love has found historically visible expression. In the concrete history of Jesus Christ, which is the history of the full self-communication of God to human being and of human being's full acceptance of it, God's gift of himself has appeared in the world in such a way as to be incontrovertible.[14] In particular, in the radical obedience to the Father and solidarity with the human race that Jesus exhibits in going to the cross, we see the depth of the love of God, on the one hand, and the depth of the human response required, on the other. In the personal relationship with Jesus that is foundational in Christian faith, but that, according to Rahner, has hitherto gone relatively unnoticed and has been markedly undeveloped in Christian theology — including his own theology — Rahner argues that this concrete history of Jesus comes to have a real and total life-giving impact upon our concrete histories.[15] Although the theme is not fully developed in his theology, this moment of subjective realization would appear to be grounded, for Rahner, in the work of the Spirit, which is, according to the conceptuality of *the Trinity*, at least to bring the truth of God's self-offering in history into all human life in such a way as to determine present and future existential experience, and, in particular, to open such human existence up in love to the pervasive mystery of grace.

Thus Jesus Christ becomes the focal point of the doctrine of the divine self-communication in Rahner's theology; but in itself, this self-communication is a more comprehensive reality that cannot itself be compressed, as it were, into the structures of Christology. Because of the absence of any doctrine of Christ as our representative, furthermore, and because of Rahner's denial that the event of the cross can be said to effect our salvation in any decisive sense — since it rather *reveals* salvation as something already presupposed in the sheer fact of God's universal free and forgiving self-communication — Rahner's theology cannot be said to

---

13. Wilhelm Thüsing, in Karl Rahner and Wilhelm Thüsing, *A New Christology*, tr. D. Smith and V. Green (London: Burns and Oates, 1980), pp. 60, 108ff.

14. Rahner, "Reconciliation and Vicarious Representation," p. 262.

15. Rahner, "The Christian Understanding of Redemption," pp. 248-51.

be Christocentric in the sense current in much modern theology. Christ is central in Rahner inasmuch and insofar as he provides for us the definitive expression or revelation of the love of God and of the human response to that love in the incarnation, but Christ is neither so central that the *whole* of God's loving disposition toward us is encapsulated in him, nor so central that the question of *our own* response to the love of God becomes effectively peripheral to the theological task. Rather, for Rahner, the human response to God, grounded in the communication of the Holy Spirit, and therefore precisely *not* restricted to the Christological question, is of basic theological importance.

To say all of this is simply to say the same thing that was said at the outset, namely, that, for Rahner, all theology must be explicitly or implicitly a theology of the spiritual life, or, at the very least, a theology that relates to the spiritual life. From this, however, follows an important conclusion. Since the human response to God is itself the gift of grace — since it is, in Rahner's phrase, "borne by God" in his self-communication[16] — and since the divine self-communication to us at this level is expressly defined as the gift of the Holy Spirit, Rahner's theology must be conceived to be primarily and decisively a theology of the Holy Spirit.

Rahner's trinitarian axiom concerning the unity of the economic with the immanent Trinity must be read and understood against this background. Rather than affirming, for example, in post-Barthian fashion that God is in himself no other than who he is in Jesus Christ,[17] Rahner's intention is to stress in more modest terms simply that the doctrine of the Trinity is a "mystery of salvation," and therefore that its content is to be conceived as bearing directly on the question of salvation as he conceives it. In fact, as anyone who even superficially peruses the contents of the *Theological Investigations* must confess, Rahner is almost completely disinterested in the question of the immanent Trinity, except insofar as he wishes to maintain that it is the reality of God *himself,* and not some created intermediary, which is given to us in the incarnation and in the experience of grace, and therefore that it is God himself who grounds the human approach to God. Otherwise, we could not with any integrity speak of the *self*-communication of God, or maintain with any consistency in our the-

---

16. Rahner, *Foundations,* p. 128.

17. Rahner characterizes this tradition, as expressed, e.g., in the notion of the suffering of God in the suffering of Christ, as "Neo-Chalcedonian," and characterizes his own position by contrast as a (reinterpreted) "pure Chalcedonism" in which the radical interpretation of the *communicatio idiomatum* given in the former is resisted. Karl Rahner, "Jesus Christ — The Meaning of Life," in *Theological Investigations,* vol. 21, pp. 213-15.

ology that God himself, the incomprehensible ground and origin whom we call Father, is with us in his Son Jesus Christ, and that in the gift of the Holy Spirit in the innermost self, we really have to do with this same God and no other. All of this is of enormous theological importance, though, to be fair, none of it can be said to be new; what is extraordinary, rather, about Rahner's doctrine of the Trinity is quite simply that this is as far as his exposition goes. Despite all the taking up of the Rahnerian trinitarian axiom mentioned above in recent trinitarian speculation, Rahner himself distinctly resists the temptation to move on the basis of the presupposed unity of economic with immanent Trinity in the direction of a theological development of the immanent mystery of the Trinity — a temptation that has so evidently been succumbed to in other quarters. For Rahner himself, the Trinity really is mystery, so that the closer we come to it and the more it is communicated to us, the greater the mystery by definition must become.[18]

The second question posed at the outset can now be addressed, concerning the relevance of Rahner's trinitarianism to the question of religious pluralism and interreligious dialogue. An intriguing comment by his friend and colleague Herbert Vorgrimler can serve as the introduction to our discussion at this point. Rahner paid increasing attention to dialogue with other religions toward the end of his life, and in particular to dialogue with Islam. According to Vorgrimler, one of the areas of Rahner's theology that could be truly pioneering in the dialogue with Islam — if only someone were willing to develop it further in this direction — is Rahner's doctrine of the Trinity.[19] Given Islam's insistence that God is one, and its correlative insistence that God neither begets, nor is begotten, this may appear a rather surprising judgment. It is, after all, precisely in the doctrine of the Trinity that Christian and Islamic theology come most sharply into conflict.

There are, however, a number of features of Rahner's conception of the Trinity that bear out Vorgrimler's suggestion. First of all, Rahner's whole approach to the doctrine of the Trinity represents an attempt to deal with its problems and possibilities in terms of the human experience of God. It is axiomatic to Rahner that this experience of God is given to and open to all human beings, without exception. In Rahner's view, therefore, there is from the beginning a point of contact between the Muslim and the Christian, or between the Hindu or the atheist and the Christian, in that all alike

---

18. Cf. Karl Rahner, "The Concept of Mystery in Catholic Theology," in Rahner, *Theological Investigations*, vol. 4, pp. 36-73.

19. Vorgrimler, p. 120.

have an immediate relation to God at the center of their being. Recognizing the presence of God in others, including in those of another religious persuasion, therefore comes to be fundamental to the task of dialogue. While Rahner would insist that in Jesus Christ we have the definitive expression of the truth of God's love, and indeed the incarnation of the divine *Logos* of trinitarian conceptuality, he would also insist that one can adequately understand what this means only from the standpoint of the more general theological anthropology he develops, which he employs in the context of interreligious dialogue.

Secondly, given the recognition of the fact that all alike, Jew and Gentile, Christian and Muslim, believer and unbeliever, are recipients of God's free and forgiving self-communication, a Rahnerian approach to interreligious dialogue would maintain that instead of dealing with others in the stark terms of lost and saved, the ungraced and the graced, one is bound to deal with other human beings as equally beloved of God and equally graced by him, but as having *recognized* and *accepted* the divine self-communication to varying degrees. The whole human race is, for Rahner, arranged along a continuum constituted by the extent to which the love of God in his self-giving is known or acknowledged, or perhaps alternatively lived in a life of love without any explicitly "religious" consciousness in the usual sense of that term. The point of dialogue can therefore be seen to be defined by the need to discern the presence, the love, the voice of God in others, rather than by the need to convince others or to convert them to one's own faith or theology, while such dialogue can be said to become fundamental to the task of Christian theology in general. Since the experience of God is at the heart of everything, including theology, the point of doing theology is simply to enter more deeply into the mystery of his presence. Such must then be the overriding priority in any dialogue with those of other religions.

Thirdly, however, Rahner is emphatic that the content of Christian faith as believed and proclaimed in the Catholic tradition is the truth, that the God of Christian revelation is the true God, and that the fullness of religious experience implies a recognition of these facts. There is therefore nonetheless a clear evangelical task facing the Church in an age of religious pluralism, a task that relates in Rahner's theology not to any prepacked missionary zeal taken from his Jesuit training, but to the simplest affirmation of his theological anthropology that human being is the event of the divine self-communication. It is precisely the *self*-communication of God, Rahner argues, that is distinctive of the Christian doctrine of God over against other religious concepts of God: God, according to Christian teaching, is the unfathomable one who relates to us by giving us himself in Word and Spirit, and not through created intermediaries. Therefore, the task of interreligious dialogue also imposes upon the Christian the responsibility to proclaim the gospel, at least in the sense of bringing to light the basic truth that God is truly present in and to human beings. At some point in such dialogue, it would presumably be appropriate to make the point that this happens in the twin modalities of Word and Spirit, incarnation and grace, and not only in the basic experience of human self-transcendence in truth and love. There is, therefore, a task of evangelization emerging from Rahner's theology that has to be undertaken in an age of religious pluralism, just as there is also a basic task of listening to and learning from others. Both tasks, however, according to the Rahnerian conception, derive from the same absolute point of theological intensity, the fact of the divine self-communication to human beings as objects of God's love.

The strengths of such an approach are relatively clear: a positive point of common concern and experience is postulated that provides a basis for discussion and real dialogue. Although those of other faiths or none might find the designation "anonymous Christians" offensive, the opening Rahner attempts to provide for a sympathetic approach by the Church to other religious bodies, whether Mosque, Synagogue, or Temple, and *vice versa,* is welcome. On a more pastoral level, the increasing numbers of couples in our society who have undertaken interfaith, and not just interchurch, marriages might also find much in the Rahnerian view that is helpful. From the standpoint of Christian faith and pastoral concerns, the problem of conscience that stems from the view that all who do not confess the name of Christ are irretrievably damned is also dealt with, even if, at the end of the day, the question of a *universal* salvation must be left to God.

On the other hand, a number of weaknesses in Rahner's approach need to be recognized. First of all, it is difficult to resist the implication from certain biblical texts that Rahner's view of the general self-communication of God, such that God becomes a constitutive principle of human being as such, is a distortion of the biblical view that human beings are by nature alienated from God. This in itself would not cause great difficulties in the task of interreligious dialogue, since this fact is also recognized and dealt with in various ways by all the great religions, but it does raise certain doubts concerning Rahner's basic starting point in his theological anthropology. Is it, in short, possible to maintain that God is close to all, so close that his presence is almost indistinguishable from the self, in view of the biblical teaching that all alike are objects of divine wrath? The fact that in Rahner the God of wrath has entirely given place to the

God of love may be theologically welcome from a certain perspective, but can it be justified in biblical terms? Rahner himself does not provide such a justification, and it must be questioned whether one could ever be provided from strict exegesis of either the Old or the New Testaments. At the very least, one must say that while there are biblical themes relating to the *imago dei*, for example, that lend support to his position, there are plenty of others that do not.

Secondly, there is an area of unclarity in what Rahner has to say concerning the theology of grace. It is only possible to maintain the position outlined *vis-à-vis* religious pluralism and interreligious dialogue on the basis of the presupposition that grace is to be conceived pneumatologically, and as detachable in some way from the Christ-event. There is a strong sense in New Testament pneumatology, however, and indeed in the Christian theological tradition in general, that the gift of the Spirit is something that flows from the Christ-event, and that is of decisive importance precisely because it is an eschatological event, something that ruptures the previous continuities of natural human existence, and that rather fulfills the final purposes of God for human existence. Admittedly, the eschatological sense that the Holy Spirit is a deposit that carries us along to the future consummation is clearly present in Rahner's theology, but what is missing is any real sense that this gift flows from who Jesus Christ is and what he has done for us in his concrete existence. When the Jesus of the fourth Gospel speaks of pneumatological rivers of living water that fulfill eschatological expectation and quench our spiritual thirst, the evangelist comments that these life-giving waters were not given until Jesus had been glorified (John 7:39). While this is, on a whole, a curiously underdeveloped theme in Christian pneumatology, one cannot ultimately bypass it, as Rahner appears to do, without thereby sacrificing something distinctive in the Christian conception of the Spirit. The fact that the Spirit appears, for Rahner, to be given fundamentally at creation, although tenable theologically, appears to conflict with the links in Scripture and tradition that are made both between Pentecost and Calvary and between the Messianic age and the life of the world to come. Although Rahner develops a strong pneumatology, or a strongly pneumatological theology, his position is inadequate and at times ambiguous precisely because it is unclear what the connection is between Christ and the Spirit — or indeed, if there is any connection. In a theology that intends to be trinitarian, this is a peculiar omission.

Perhaps it is expecting too much of any theology to provide a seamless, watertight web of thought that can hold out indefinitely against all theological storms that may arise. Rahner's theology was not primarily intended to provide a new development of the doctrine of the Trinity, nor to undergird a theology of interreligious dialogue; rather, it was constructed with an express view to the renewal of Roman Catholic theology in the twentieth century. It is clear that to this extent, Rahner achieved a very great deal; Roman Catholic theology in the contemporary context is a vastly different and a vastly stronger thing than it might otherwise have been without his influence. Rahner has also provided enormous stimulus to the ecumenical enterprise, and, as the above reflections may indicate, to those Christians engaged in dialogue with people of other faiths. However, on a number of grounds, Rahner's theology can be found to be wanting, and wanting precisely a more adequately conceived and developed trinitarian structure. If in his doctrine of the Trinity Rahner has contributed significantly to the development of modern theology, it is here too, in his doctrine of the Trinity, that his most glaring theological inadequacies can be seen. Nevertheless, his achievement in opening up theology to the presence of God as a trinitarian reality and his corresponding insistence that the doctrine of the Trinity can retain its function and meaning in theology only to the extent that it is properly conceived as a mystery of salvation have rendered a permanent service to Christian theology, and one that ought not to be dismissed superficially.

· 10 ·

Jürgen Moltmann's
The Trinity and the Kingdom of God
and the Question of Pluralism

RICHARD BAUCKHAM

As its title declares, *The Trinity and the Kingdom of God* is not just a book about the Trinity, but a book about the Trinity in relation to God's kingdom. For, as Moltmann says, "Theology is never concerned with the actual *existence* of a God. It is interested solely in the *rule* of this God in heaven and on earth" (TKG, p. 191).[1] The central problem the book addresses is therefore not the problem of the doctrine of the Trinity, presented as the intellectual conundrum it is sometimes made to appear. Certainly, the major task of the book is "the task of revising the church's doctrine of the Trinity on the basis of the Bible" (TKG, p. 65). But the doctrine of the Trinity, for Moltmann, is not the problem; properly understood, it is the solution.

The problem is that of the rule of God and human freedom. Succinctly put in the words Moltmann quotes from Ernst Bloch: "Where the great Lord of the universe reigns, there is no room for liberty" (TKG, p. 203). Actually this is two problems. There is the problem that if God is absolute monarch, we are his slaves: the divine sovereignty leaves no room for human freedom. Of course, this is a classic theological problem, but Moltmann is not concerned here with the soteriological debate about predestination and free will. He is more concerned with the modern percep-

---

1. References to TKG are to page numbers of J. Moltmann's *The Trinity and the Kingdom of God,* tr. M. Kohl (London: SCM Press, 1981).

tion, at the root of modern atheism, of the incompatibility of human freedom with belief in an almighty, sovereign God (TKG, p. 203). But since the modern rejection of God in the name of human freedom has often coincided with the rejection of political autocracies in the name of human freedom, there is a second problem about the rule of God and human freedom. This is that the rule of God, as absolute monarch of the world, has functioned in religious history as the model and legitimation for absolute rule by human monarchs on earth. Divine domination authorizes human domination at the expense of human freedom: "The notion of a divine monarchy in heaven and on earth . . . generally provides the justification for earthly domination — religious, moral, patriarchal or political domination — and makes it a hierarchy, a 'holy rule'. The idea of an almighty ruler of the universe everywhere requires abject servitude, because it points to complete dependency in all spheres of life" (TKG, pp. 191-192). What Moltmann calls "monotheistic monarchianism" — the one God as sole ruler of the universe — both constitutes the first problem and gives rise to the second. He spells this out in a critique of both "political monotheism" and "clerical monotheism" (TKG, pp. 192-202).

The issue in *The Trinity and the Kingdom of God* is therefore freedom, not pluralism. But insofar as pluralism seems to be a necessary concomitant of freedom, we may well find Moltmann's discussion relevant to the theme of pluralism. If God's rule means the elimination or coercion of human freedom, both by his direct rule and by his delegated rule through human autocracies, political and ecclesiastical, then it enforces uniformity and suppresses pluralism. Moltmann himself points out that this was the appeal that Christianity, interpreted as "monotheistic monarchianism," had in the Roman Empire. By offering a universal and uniform religion — worship of the one universal ruler in heaven to whom the Roman emperor as universal ruler on earth corresponded — it seemed "a persuasive solution to the many problems of a multi-national and multi-religious society" (TKG, p. 131).

Moltmann uses the term "monotheism" as the opposite of trinitarianism. So Karl Barth's claim that the doctrine of the Trinity is "Christian monotheism" (quoted in TKG, pp. 63, 140) is by no means a recommendation of Barth's doctrine of the Trinity, in Moltmann's eyes. Moltmann might have been less open to misunderstanding had he used the term "unitarianism" rather than "monotheism," but he is rather deliberately contrasting the Christian — fully trinitarian — concept of God with non-Christian monotheistic concepts and with Christian theological views that have allowed such concepts priority over the biblical Christian understanding of God as Trinity.

Such Christian monotheism occurs when either the Greek philosophical notion of God as supreme substance or the modern idealistic concept of God as absolute subject is given priority over the trinitarian differentiation in God. But the divine unicity — whether as substance or subject — is closely connected with the divine monarchy. The one God is sole ruler, and so other features of classical theism of which Moltmann has long been critical — divine impassibility and the related view of the God-world relationship as a purely one-way relationship: God affects the world but cannot be affected by the world — are implicated in Christian monotheism. What Moltmann opposes comes to classic expression in his account of Barth's trinitarian doctrine, making his disagreement with Barth pivotal to his whole argument. In Barth the sovereignty of God and the notion of God as absolute subject coincide, and the doctrine of the Trinity is understood as an interpretation of this: "God reveals himself as Lord" (see TKG, pp. 63, 140-141). Inevitably the Trinity is collapsed into the threefold repetition of a single subject. It is instructive to observe what Moltmann sees as the mistake here. The sole sovereignty of the one God is given priority over the divine Trinity (TKG, p. 63) — and the result is Barth's alleged "modalism" (only one divine subject in three modes of being). Divine monarchy entails unitarianism. By contrast Moltmann wants to give priority to the Trinity and to understand the rule of God differently in its light. Social trinitarianism will then entail something other than divine monarchy.

Moltmann's criticism of Christian monotheism is both that it makes the rule of God incompatible with human freedom and also that it is insufficiently Christian, that is, insufficiently trinitarian. The basis of the doctrine of the Trinity is the history of Jesus Christ, which the New Testament tells as a narrative of relationships between three divine persons. So the nonnegotiable starting point for trinitarian doctrine is that three divine subjects relate to each other in salvation history. From this starting point develops a doctrine of the Trinity that we can briefly summarize, for our present purposes, in five closely related points:

(1) The relationship between God and the world is a two-way relationship, in which God is affected by the world as well as affecting it. Moltmann's understanding of the cross, from which his trinitarian thought originally developed, is central here, in that it entails divine passibility, though this is by no means the only way in which the God-world relationship is reciprocal. The two-way relationship means, of course, that God himself has a history. As far as technical trinitarian theology goes, it means that, while Moltmann in *The Trinity and the Kingdom of God* no longer denies the distinction between the immanent Trinity and the economic

Trinity, as he had in earlier work, the relation between the two has itself to be two-way, not, as in classical theology, one-way.

(2) Moltmann's social doctrine of the Trinity conceives of God as three divine subjects in interpersonal relationship with each other — a fellowship of love. Their unity does not precede their distinction, but consists in their community together, which Moltmann, in one of the finest sections of the book, describes by an interpretation of the doctrine of the trinitarian perichoresis supplemented by a doctrine of trinitarian manifestations. The life of God is a life of living fellowship and a process of expression of the divine life through mutual manifestation (TKG, pp. 174-76).

(3) God's trinitarian history with the world is a history in which the three divine persons relate both to each other and to the world. It is not a history in which a fixed order of trinitarian relationships appears, but a history of changing trinitarian relationships, in which the relations between the persons both affect the world and are affected by the world. It is a history in which the world is included within the trinitarian relationships of the three divine persons.

(4) Thus the Trinity is a process of living relationships of love, between the three persons and open to the inclusion of the world.

(5) This doctrine of the Trinity makes no use of the notion of rule. It is true that, at one of the points where Moltmann is slavishly and unnecessarily faithful to features of traditional trinitarian theology, he does retain the traditional idea of the Father as sole source of Godhead (the so-called monarchy of the Father). But he diverges from tradition in limiting this element of subordination to what he calls the "constitution" of the Trinity, allowing it no place in the perichoretic relations among the three: "Here the three Persons are equal; they live and are manifested in one another and through one another" (TKG, p. 176). The notion of divine monarchy is not used to explain the Trinity; the Trinity itself must reveal the meaning of the kingdom of God.

Of course, Moltmann's point is not to substitute a divine oligarchy of three for a divine monarchy of one. This would be of no benefit to human freedom. The point is that God is defined as love rather than as lordship. God relates to the world in love — both acting in love and suffering in love — and can do so because God's own being is an open fellowship of love. If God's rule is given priority in the doctrine of God, freedom is eliminated. But if the Trinity is given priority, then God's rule can only be the rule of love, which is compatible with freedom just as love is compatible with freedom (or rather: constitutive of freedom).

So far so good (it seems to me). But the two more specific ways in which Moltmann then proceeds to work out the implications of his doctrine of the Trinity seem to me more problematic. They are two quite different and distinct lines of argument:

(1) Moltmann proposes the trinitarian fellowship of the three divine persons as a model for true human community, which is both to reflect and to participate in God's own trinitarian life. There are two elements to this argument. First, in a development of the idea of the divine image in humanity, Moltmann finds the image of God not in the human individual in his or her isolated subjectivity reflecting the lone divine Subject, but in human community reflecting the interpersonal life of the social Trinity. Karl Rahner's argument that the modern meaning of "person" requires that God be conceived as one person is trenchantly (and with justification) criticized for presupposing modern bourgeois cultivation of the individual (TKG, pp. 145, 155-56; quote at p. 156):

> It is inescapably obvious that, for the sake of the identity of the self-communicating divine subject, Rahner has to surrender the interpersonal relations of the triune God. And with this, of course, the prototypical character of the triune God for the personal fellowship of men and women in the church and in society collapses too.

The trinitarian perichoresis, in which the divine persons are themselves in their distinction from and (equally) at-oneness with each other, provides a pattern of personhood as that of individuals in relationship (TKG, p. 199):

> the image of God must not merely be sought for in human individuality; we must look for it with equal seriousness in human sociality. . . . If we take our bearings from the Christian doctrine of the Trinity, personalism and socialism cease to be antitheses and are seen to be derived from a common foundation. The Christian doctrine of the Trinity compels us to develop social personalism or personal socialism.

However, the argument is not merely against individualism, but also against relationships of inequality and domination. This is the second element in the argument, though Moltmann does not readily distinguish the two elements, since he takes it for granted that the possessive individualism that conceives of the person as a self-disposing center of action independent of others (TKG, p. 145) is closely akin to the practice of lordship, which relates to other persons only by way of power to dispose of them (TKG, p. 198). So here it becomes important that the perichoretic unity of the three divine persons is a nonhierarchical fellowship of open love (TKG, p. 157):

> If . . . we have to recognize the unity of the triune God in the perichoretic at-oneness of the Father, the Son and the Holy Spirit, then this does not correspond to the solitary human subject in his relationship to himself; nor does it correspond, either, to a human subject in his claim to lordship over the world. It only corresponds to a human fellowship of people without privileges and without subordinances.

Thus, both in the church and in society (TKG, pp. 157-58, 198-200), the trinitarian image is found in *community*, which domination destroys but open acceptance of the other and participation in the life of the other creates. So, in place of the concept of God as divine monarch providing the prototype for human domination, at the expense of freedom, the social Trinity provides a model for human community in which people are free for each other and find freedom in relationship with each other.

Attractive as it is (and paralleled in the work of other contemporary theologians), there seem to me to be serious problems with this line of argument. Moltmann is trying to hold together the two rather different ideas: that (a) the life of the Trinity is an interpersonal fellowship in which we, by grace, participate, and (b) the life of the Trinity provides the proto-type on which human life should be modeled (for the combination of the two ideas, see especially TKG, pp. 157-58). I doubt whether the combination is really successful. According to the first idea, we experience the trinitarian relationships from the inside, and from the standpoint of a specific, differ-entiated relationship to each of the three persons: we know Jesus as God become our fellow-human, brother, and friend, we know God the Father as his and our Father, and we know the Holy Spirit as indwelling life and power. According to the second idea, however, we are invited to stand outside this participation in the Trinity and our specific relationships to the three persons, and to view the Trinity as an external model that human relationships should reflect. This view of our relationship to the Trinity has no biblical basis (significantly, the New Testament does not use the idea of the image of God in this way), and is only artificially combined with the first idea.

The two ideas would be fairly easily compatible were we to think of the Trinity as simply like a group of three friends who include us in their friendship as yet more friends. In that case, it would be natural to think that the kind of relationship (friendship) enjoyed by the original group of three friends is the kind of relationship the new members of the circle have with each other, since what has happened is that the friendship circle has been expanded. But it is misleading to think in that way of the Trinity and our participation in the life of the Trinity. It obscures the fact that we enjoy highly differentiated relationship to the three divine persons. We do not relate to Jesus the incarnate Son in the same way as we relate to God the Father, though we can think of both in interpersonal terms, while our mode of relationship to the Spirit is not interpersonal at all. The Spirit, by indwelling us in a uniquely divine way for which human personal relationships do not provide an analogy, enables our personal relationship with the Son and the Father, but is not experienced by us as personal other in interpersonal relationship. This is not to deny the subjectivity of the Spirit, but means that we experience that subjectivity as inspiring our own subjectivity, not as vis-à-vis our own subjectivity in personal otherness. The point of Christian talk of the Trinity is to ground precisely this highly differentiated threefold relationship in which Christians come to know God and to participate in the divine life. It means that true human community comes about not as an image of the trinitarian fellowship, but as the Spirit makes us like Jesus in his community with the Father and with others. The way in which this enables freedom needs developing in a different way from this particular line of Moltmann's argument.

A related problem with the argument is that, just as it neglects the differentiated character of our relationship with the trinitarian persons, so it neglects the differentiated character of the relationships of the trinitarian persons themselves, which must be, in a way we cannot begin to comprehend, the basis for their ability to relate in a differentiated way to us. The idea of the social Trinity as a model for human community encourages us to think of the differences in the trinitarian relationships — the different ways in which the Father relates to the Son, the Son to the Father, the Father to the Spirit, the Son to the Spirit, the Spirit to each of the other two persons — as no more significant than the differences in human relationships within the kind of community Moltmann envisages. Or to put the same point another way: it encourages us to apply the term "person" as univocally to the three divine persons as we do to human persons. But this is precisely what Moltmann himself warns should not be done in his useful section on "the trinitarian principle of uniqueness" (TKG, pp. 188-90, quoted at pp. 189-90):

The 'three Persons' are different, not merely in their relations to one another, but also in respect of their character as Persons, even if the

161

person is to be understood in his relations, and not apart from them. If we wanted to remain specific, we should have to use a different concept in each case when applying the word 'person' to the Father, the Son and the Spirit. The Holy Spirit is not a person in the same, identical sense as the Son; and neither of them is a person in the same, identical sense as the Father. Their description as divine Persons in the plural already shows a tendency towards modalism in itself. For the generic term hypostasis or person stresses what is the same and in common, not what is particular and different about them.

Essentially, this is a correct and necessary safeguard against the illegitimate anthropomorphism that so easily infects discussions of the Trinity, including Moltmann's. The doctrine of the Trinity means that God is God in three inconceivably different ways. We should certainly not reduce these three to three ways in which a single, identical divine subject repeats or relates to himself: to make this point is the merit of Moltmann's argument for social trinitarianism. But we should also beware of supposing that the subjectivity of each is equally analogous to human subjectivity. Rather, each must transcend human subjectivity in a quite different and distinctive way, which we can glimpse only in observing the consequence that incarnation is appropriate to the Son, not to the Father or the Spirit, while inspiration and indwelling in the Word are appropriate to the Spirit, not to the Father or the Son. The concept of the Trinity as a society on which human society can be modeled flattens these trinitarian differences and reduces our sense of the otherness of God, which precisely the doctrine of the Trinity should heighten.

(2) Moltmann's second line of argument as to the implications of his doctrine of the Trinity is that pursued in the final section of *The Trinity and the Kingdom of God:* "The Trinitarian Doctrine of Freedom." Here Moltmann, inspired by Joachim of Fiore's trinitarian theology of history, develops a trinitarian understanding of the kingdom of God in which three aspects of the kingdom, appropriated to the Father, the Son, and the Spirit, relate to three forms or stages of human freedom. Unlike Joachim, Moltmann does not regard the kingdom of the Father, the kingdom of the Son, and the kingdom of the Spirit, with the three forms of freedom that correspond to them, as successive chronological periods, but as "strata in the concept of freedom" (TKG, p. 223). The three forms of freedom are always all present in Christian experience of freedom, but there is also a trend from the first to the third (TKG, pp. 223-24).

In the kingdom of the Father, in which God is Creator and Lord of his creation, people experience the freedom of being God's servants, which liberates them from subjection to anything other than the sole lordship of God (TKG, p. 219). (It is interesting to notice that here — but virtually nowhere else in the book — Moltmann acknowledges that the notion of obedience to God as Lord need not be oppressive, but has a liberating aspect.) In the kingdom of the Son, the servants of the Lord become the children of the Father, and enjoy the liberty of personal and intimate relationship to the Father and of participation in his kingdom (TKG, pp. 219-20). In the kingdom of the Spirit, the servants and the children become God's friends, a relationship that "becomes possible when people know themselves in God and God in them" (TKG, p. 220), and that is characterized by boldness and confidence in prayer (TKG, pp. 220-21).

This scheme, which one could have wished to see developed at greater length, is certainly suggestive with regard to the dimensions of freedom in relation to God, but as a *trinitarian* scheme it is somewhat problematic. The relationship of each "kingdom" and form of freedom to its respective divine person is certainly to be understood as a form of "appropriation" (to use traditional trinitarian terminology). In other words, Moltmann does not mean that each form of freedom is a relationship only to the particular trinitarian person to whose "kingdom" he assigns it, but he does think of the trinitarian person in question as distinctively active in creating or enabling the form of freedom in question. Thus, for example, it is obvious that the freedom of sons and daughters of God is relationship with the Father, but it is the Son who opens up this relationship for people. But whether these three appropriations can really be sustained is dubious. For example, in the New Testament, Christ's redemptive work liberates people from slavery to sin so that they may be obedient to God, and this obedience is at least as characteristically that of servants of *Christ* the Lord as it is that of servants of God the Father. But most problematic is the role of the Spirit, who in Pauline theology makes possible our participation in Jesus' relationship of sonship to God (Rom. 8:15-17; Gal. 4:6-7), whereas in John 15:13-15 (cited by Moltmann: TKG, p. 220) it is Jesus who makes his disciples his friends, and the indwelling of the Spirit is not mentioned, even if implicit. To distinguish, even as a matter of appropriation, the Son as the source of the freedom of children of God and the Spirit as the source of the freedom of friends of God seems unfounded. In both cases, the Spirit, as the enabler of relationship, gives the inner freedom of relating to another divine person: to the Father as Father, to Jesus as friend. If we are to think of an aspect of freedom that should be associated specifically with the Spirit, it is the freedom of being "led by the Spirit" (Gal. 5:18), which makes goodness not only conformity to the will of another, but also the inner, spontaneous desire of our own hearts.

Rather than trying to modify Joachim's scheme, it would be better to focus on the differentiated structure of the Christian experience of God, in which — to use one set of metaphors — we know God in three dimensions: as God above us (the Father), alongside us (Jesus, the Son), and within us (the Spirit). The fact that this is the structure of God's *love* for us excludes the domination that eliminates freedom. But also the fact that God's love for us has *this* structure excludes the merely paternalistic care that inhibits freedom. The structure gives Christian freedom three poles between which it takes shape: authority with belonging, solidarity, spontaneity. The correlation of these three poles with the three trinitarian persons is not to be pressed too far, but they do indicate a trinitarian shape to the Christian experience of freedom. Each of the three would need careful exposition to explode the myth that God's lordship is incompatible with human freedom and to show how, on the contrary, it enables human freedom.

Contributors

GARY BADCOCK is Meldrum Lecturer in Dogmatic Theology at New College, University of Edinburgh. He has written a theology of the Holy Spirit called *Light of Truth and Fire of Love* and is the editor of *Disruption to Diversity: Edinburgh Divinity 1846-1896*.

RICHARD BAUCKHAM is Professor of New Testament at St. Mary's College, University of St. Andrews. He is the author of *The Theology of Jürgen Moltmann* and *The Bible in Politics: How to Read the Bible Politically*.

HENRI BLOCHER is Professor at the Faculté Libre de Théologie Évangélique de Vaux-sur-Seine, near Paris. He is the author of *Le mal et la croix* and *In the Beginning*.

GERALD BRAY is Professor of Anglican Theology at Beeson Divinity School, Samford University, Birmingham, Alabama. He is the author of *The Doctrine of God, Biblical Interpretation: Past and Present* and the editor of the Anglican quarterly *The Churchman*.

COLIN GUNTON is Professor of Christian Doctrine at King's College, University of London. He is the author of *The One, the Three and the Many: God, Creation and the Culture of Modernity* and the editor of *The Cambridge Companion to Christian Doctrine*.

TREVOR HART is Professor of Systematic Theology at the University of St. Andrews. He is the author of *Faith Thinking: The Dynamics of Chris-*

tian Theology and the editor of the forthcoming *Dictionary of Historical Theology.*

LESSLIE NEWBIGIN was formerly a bishop in the Church of South India and a teacher at Selly Oak Colleges in Birmingham. He is the author of *Foolishness to the Greeks: The Gospel and Western Culture* and *The Gospel in a Pluralist Society.*

ROLAND POUPIN is a pastor of the Église Reformée in southern France. Previously he lectured in the history of Christian thought and theology at the European Bible Institute in Lamorlaye, France. He is the author of *Les Cathares, l'âme et la réincarnation.*

KEVIN J. VANHOOZER is Senior Lecturer in Theology and Religious Studies at New College, University of Edinburgh. He is the author of *Biblical Narrative in the Philosophy of Paul Ricoeur: A Study in Hermeneutics and Theology* and *Is There a Meaning in this Text? The Bible, the Reader, and the Morality of Literary Knowledge.*

STEPHEN WILLIAMS is Professor of Systematic Theology at Union Theological College, Belfast. He is the author of *Revelation and Reconciliation: A Window on Modernity.*